T0318905

Cambridge Elements

Elements in Eighteenth-Century Connections
edited by
Eve Tavor Bannet
University of Oklahoma
Markman Ellis
Queen Mary University of London

READING WITH THE BURNEYS

Patronage, Paratext, and Performance

Sophie Coulombeau
University of York

CAMBRIDGE
UNIVERSITY PRESS

CAMBRIDGE
UNIVERSITY PRESS

Shaftesbury Road, Cambridge CB2 8EA, United Kingdom

One Liberty Plaza, 20th Floor, New York, NY 10006, USA

477 Williamstown Road, Port Melbourne, VIC 3207, Australia

314–321, 3rd Floor, Plot 3, Splendor Forum, Jasola District Centre,
New Delhi – 110025, India

103 Penang Road, #05–06/07, Visioncrest Commercial, Singapore 238467

Cambridge University Press is part of Cambridge University Press & Assessment,
a department of the University of Cambridge.

We share the University's mission to contribute to society through the pursuit of
education, learning and research at the highest international levels of excellence.

www.cambridge.org
Information on this title: www.cambridge.org/9781009532945

DOI: 10.1017/9781009439480

First published 2024

A catalogue record for this publication is available from the British Library.

ISBN 978-1-009-53294-5 Hardback
ISBN 978-1-009-43951-0 Paperback
ISSN 2632-5578 (online)
ISSN 2632-556X (print)

Reading with the Burneys

Patronage, Paratext, and Performance

Elements in Eighteenth-Century Connections

DOI: 10.1017/9781009439480
First published online: June 2024

Sophie Coulombeau
University of York

Author for correspondence: Sophie Coulombeau,
Sophie.coulombeau@york.ac.uk

Abstract: This Element offers a multidimensional study of reading practice and sibling rivalry in late eighteenth-century Britain. The case study is the Aberdeen student and disgraced thief Charles Burney's treatment of *Evelina* (1778), the debut novel of his sister Frances Burney. Coulombeau uses Charles's manuscript poetry, letters, and marginalia, alongside illustrative prints and circulating library archives, to tell the story of how he attempted to control *Evelina's* reception in an effort to bolster his own socio-literary status. Uniting approaches drawn from literary studies, biography, bibliography, and the history of the book, the Element enriches scholarly understanding of the reception of Frances Burney's fiction, with broader implications for studies of gender, class, kinship, and reading in this period. This title is also available as Open Access on Cambridge Core.

Keywords: Frances Burney, Charles Burney, reading practices, *Evelina*, libraries

ISBNs: 9781009532945 (HB), 9781009439510 (PB), 9781009439480 (OC)
ISSNs: 2632-5578 (online), 2632-556X (print)

Contents

Introduction

In the summer of 1779, a young theology student called Charles Burney (1757–1817) wrote from Aberdeen to his older sister Frances (1752–1840) in London. His subject was the local reception of her debut novel, *Evelina: Or, a Young Lady's Entrance into the World*, first published in London by Thomas Lowndes in January 1778. Charles's description of *Evelina*'s journey around Aberdeen is one of those first-hand testimonies which can, if properly contextualised, change how we think about both literary history and the history of reading.

> Evelina is in Aberdeen – I have had it, from a Circulating Library, & have lent to my two angels, the Miss Willox's – The Miss Gordon's – & their Father & Mother – to Dr Gerard & Family – & now a Mrs Paul has it; an aunt of my Charmers as need I name them. I cannot tell you half the fine things which have been said about it – They are all in raptures with it – & all longing to see *you* –
>
> Dr. Gerard, the Professor of Divinity – think of that! – has read it, & admires it *of all things*! He doats upon Madame Duval –
>
> Miss Gerard is fond of Miss Mirvan – the Youths of that family have not read it yet.–
>
> Mr Gordon, the Professor of Philosophy, read it through *twice* – He thinks Sir Clement the best drawn & supported Character –
>
> Before I return it, I shall lend it all around: to all the sweet Creatures, of which this Town is full.
>
> Miss Willox is very fond of Evelina, & she and my lovely Jessy admire the Branghton Family.
>
> But the Captain is my adorable Jessy's favourite – she says that she almost killed herself with laughing –
>
> Mrs Willox is very fond of Mr Villars – Mr Willox has not read it.
>
> Mr Gordon laments that the meeting between Sir John Belmont, & Mr Villars was not made the subject of another Letter – He says, he is sure that Miss Burney's pen would have made a great deal of it –
>
> Every body is surprised at the Performance, however: – I prefixed the little sonnet, which I gave you some time since, to the set which I lent about. *That* likewise had its *admirers* – I addressed it, '*To the Female Reader*!'[1]

In this Element, I use the above testimony, alongside other sources, to make several claims about Charles Burney, Frances Burney, and more broadly the ways in which gender, class, and kinship could inflect eighteenth-century reading experiences. In doing so, I model a process I call '3D reading', which unites

---

[1] Charles Burney to Frances Burney, OSB MSS 3, Box 6, Folder 381. I date this letter to early summer by its reference in an unquoted section to James Dunbar's visit to London in May 1779. The transcript is my own, taken directly from the manuscript: this is the case for all quotations from archival sources throughout the Element.

methodological approaches from literary studies, biography, bibliography, and the history of the book to generate a deeper understanding of late eighteenth-century reading practices.

Critical Context

What, where, when, how, and why did eighteenth-century readers read? In recent years, the desire to reconstruct reading experiences of the past – an objective which James Raven calls 'the most significant and challenging dimension of the history of books' – has generated numerous methodological approaches across the field of eighteenth-century studies. Some scholars suggest that reading practices can be understood with reference to the 'manners of reading' outlined within instructional literature.[2] Others interrogate material traces of reader interaction with extant textual artefacts to offer clues as to how they were used.[3] Most agree that accounts of individuals' private reading practices gleaned from diaries, letters, and other manuscript sources remain crucial.[4] Some collaborative digital projects harness the capabilities of crowd-sourcing, web-crawling or text-mining to code, model, and analyse such accounts in new ways,[5] while others draw on the archives of eighteenth-century libraries or booksellers to develop data-driven visualisations of local, regional, and national reading habits.[6]

The 'transformative capacity' of reading is notoriously difficult to gauge.[7] For the most part, scholars still endeavour to do so by examining 'private and critical' contemporary reader responses drawn from letters and diaries.[8] Such an approach, however, raises questions around not only representativeness but also reliability. As Katie Halsey notes, life writing is an opaque, slippery, and complex genre.[9] When self-reporting ways in which a text has transformed them or others, writers may pursue multiple agendas – flattery, spite, or self-promotion, for example – which compromise the reliability of their accounts. As I show in the coming pages, a young man attempting to

---

[2] Bannet, *Eighteenth-Century Manners of Reading*; de Ritter, *Imagining Women Readers*.

[3] Jackson, *Marginalia*; Williams, *Reading It Wrong*.

[4] Ellis, 'Reading Practices'; Halsey, *Jane Austen and Her Readers*; Matthews, 'I feel the mind enlarging itself' and 'To do a little and well'.

[5] *READ-IT (Reading Europe Advanced Data Investigation Tool)*, 2018–2021, Université du Main le Mans; *Unlocking the Mary Hamilton Papers*, 2019–2023, University of Manchester.

[6] *The French Book Trade in Enlightenment Europe Project, 1769–1794*, 2015–present, University of Leeds and Western Sydney University; *Libraries, Reading Communities & Cultural Formation in the 18th Century Atlantic*, 2019–2024, University of Liverpool; *Books and Borrowing: An Analysis of Scottish Readers' Registers 1750–1830*, 2020–2024, University of Stirling.

[7] Towheed et al., *The History of Reading*, 1.   [8] Halsey, *Jane Austen and her Readers*, 14.

[9] Halsey, *Jane Austen and her Readers*, 93–4.

promote his own intellectual gifts may well declare that he is 'not in general fond of Novels', but other sources – especially the poetry he composed – may tell a different story.

One way to circumvent the problem of opaque or misleading reader testimony is to combine several disciplinary methodologies and use them to hold one another to account: an approach I term '3D reading'. This Element attempts to model such a process. I argue that by constructing a rich multidimensional case study of one unusual reader's relationship with one extraordinary text, we can gain an enhanced sense of the forms which readerly transformation may have taken. Deidre Shauna Lynch has recently shown how, during this period, 'literary reading became subject to new expectations of affective obligation and dilemmas of affective entanglement'.[10] This Element follows Lynch and others in centring the affective dimensions of eighteenth-century reading experiences, but dives deeper into one case study than traditional forms of academic publication will generally permit. The space allowed by the unique form of the Element (or 'minigraph') allows me to tell my story from a number of archival and theoretical angles.

My reader of choice is the young man who would later in life be known as the Rev. Charles Burney D.D.: schoolmaster, author, critic, clergyman, bibliomaniac, and notorious thief. Throughout his sixty years, Charles Burney demonstrated an intense acquisitive relationship with material texts, both elite and ephemeral, in manuscript and in print. More accurately termed logomania than bibliomania since it was not restricted to codices, his condition found one expression in the best-known event of Charles's life: his teenage expulsion from the University of Cambridge in 1778 for stealing ninety-two rare books from the University Library, after which he was exiled to King's College Aberdeen to finish his studies and live down his disgrace. The second achievement for which he is commonly known is the vast personal library purchased after his death in 1817 for the British Museum, part of which, as Gale Cengage's Burney Collection of Newspapers, now underpins an enormous amount of scholarly research into the history, literature, and culture of early modern Britain and America.

Despite his intriguing profile and important legacy, Charles Burney has largely been neglected by book historians and literary scholars alike. The only notable exceptions are two biographical articles by Ralph Walker written half a century ago, and multiple brief references scattered throughout biographies and collected correspondence of other, more famous, members of the Burney

---

[10] Lynch, *Loving Literature*, 24.

family.[11] In the last few years, however, Charles has begun to attract attention in his own right as a figure with much to contribute to various fields. In particular, his habits as a reader and collector have begun to receive sharp sideways glances, with Katie Lanning describing him as a 'compelling figure to study in terms of popular culture theory'[12] and Gillian Russell proposing that his 'combin[ation of] the identities of book lover and ephemerile' does not easily fit within the categories conventionally used to understand Romantic bibliomania.[13] An account of Charles's unusual relationship with *Evelina*, which I have been gradually uncovering for the last ten years, offers a timely opportunity to bring his practices as a reader and bibliophile to the forefront of literary-historical scholarship in the long eighteenth century.

The text that enables me to do so is the debut novel of Charles's elder sister, Frances Burney. *Evelina* is a polyphonic epistolary fiction which combines elements of the sentimental romance, the comic picaresque, and the novel of manners. The plot follows a naïve young girl's quest to establish her rightful parentage while navigating the pitfalls of fashionable London life. Frequently hailed as one of the most innovative and influential fictions of the long eighteenth century, it has in recent decades become a staple of university syllabi, popular with students as well as researchers. However, recent studies have mainly focused on the novel's gender politics, authorial persona, and paratexts,[14] and its reception among contemporary readers has not been sufficiently interrogated. Scholars often characterise *Evelina*'s reception as a chorus of universal acclaim, either drawing unquestioningly on Burney's own life writing[15] or repeating certain well-known compliments from other literary figures which are used as evidence of unqualified admiration.[16] Other records of reader response, which have potential to complicate and enrich this picture, remain largely unplumbed.

This Element aims to nuance our understanding of *Evelina*'s reception by describing Charles Burney's relationship to Frances's novel during the three years he spent in North East Scotland and positioning it within a broader range of reader responses within his Scottish circles and beyond. Charles's numerous manuscript letters and poems from this period provide my starting point, since

---

[11] For the articles, see Walker 'Charles Burney's Theft' and 'Charles Burney's Tour'. For biographies, see especially Scholes, *The Great Dr Burney*; Hemlow, *History*; Doody, *The Life in the Works*; and Chisholm, *Fanny Burney*. For collections of correspondence, see the works under 'List of Abbreviations'.

[12] Lanning, 'Scanner Darkly', 216. [13] Russell, *The Ephemeral Eighteenth Century*, 172.

[14] Paluchowska-Messing, *The Negotiated Image*; Kochkina *Frances Burney's Evelina*.

[15] Gallagher, *Nobody's Story*, 226; Spencer, *Kinship and the Canon*, 52–53; both of which draw on Hemlow, *History,* 102.

[16] Paluchowska-Messing, *The Negotiated Image*, 12–13.

they provide an unusually full account of his treatment of *Evelina*, both in the extract already quoted and elsewhere. I also draw on the sonnet he 'prefixed' to his sister's novel, which survives in two different versions, and on his other poems composed during this time. Furthermore, internal evidence from a 1779 third edition of *Evelina* held in the University of Aberdeen's Special Collections – which I argue is actually one of the sets circulated by Charles – demonstrates how his tactile approach to the text fostered sociable relationships across genteel Scottish society. Finally, a unique copy of *Conditions* attached to the Catalogue of an Aberdeen circulating library provides vital information within which to contextualise Charles's treatment of the set, while illustrative prints and frontispieces depicting a popular scene in *Evelina* offer a sense of the context within which he identified with the character of Mr Macartney.

The singular value of Charles Burney's testimony is that, across all these sources, he stands in several distinct yet fluid relations to *Evelina:* prefixer, reader, and loaner. By synthesising such roles, we can mutually improve our understanding of Charles Burney's reader profile, of Frances Burney's authorial reception, and of the complexity of reading practices in late eighteenth-century Britain. The case of *Evelina* in Aberdeen helps us to rethink how books might be used as objects of circulation, inscription, and exchange; how they might disseminate knowledge and pleasure, generate affective attachment, and foster social networks. In offering these insights, this Element connects the fields of literary studies, biography, bibliography, and the history of the book.

Core Claims

The Element makes three claims about Frances and Charles Burney. First, I argue that, in an attempt to rebuild his own social standing in the wake of his Cambridge disgrace, Charles offered privileged access to his sister's imaginative interiority and attempted to control how her novel was received within a reading community of his own creation. This claim extends Eve Tavor Bannet's recent illustration of how 'learned critics [might] give the character of an Author [through oral performance]'[17] to encompass *textual* self-creation. My approach also has significant implications for the topic of 'family authorship,' as addressed by Michelle Levy, Scott Krawczyk, and Hilary Havens, calling into question the terms under which such collaborations took place *post-publication* and positioning the Burney family as a crucial case study in this respect.[18]

---

[17] Bannet *Eighteenth-Century Manners of Reading*, 92.
[18] Levy, *Family Authorship*; Krawczyk, *Romantic Literary Families;* Havens, *Revising the Eighteenth-Century Novel.*

Second, I show that Charles's project was facilitated by a tendency of Frances's fiction to provoke a certain response, which I define as 'identified performance', in contemporaneous readers. Frances Burney's novels have often been used to investigate how early readers conducted acts of 'poaching' (to use Michel de Certeau's useful metaphor), especially in terms of staged and sociable readings aloud.[19] I argue, however, that her characters provoke identified performances which are not confined to closed reading sessions, but rather shape everyday textual and verbal behaviours, enabling the performer to blur the boundary between fiction and reality. While I showcase a range of case studies to demonstrate the fluidity of identified performance, my central focus is on Charles's performance of Frances's character Mr Macartney, and on his general eagerness to highlight the novel's sentimental themes to press his own amatory and material advantage.

Third, I suggest that Charles's reading practices were emphatically shaped by his status as a precarious agent within a loan economy. Despite the valuable cognate scholarship of David Allan, Mark Towsey, Jan Fergus, and Stephen Colclough,[20] little evidence currently exists about how readers considered the circulating library book as property, what rights they considered themselves to have over such an item, and the affective significance of the loan text as a mechanism for the circulation of knowledge, entertainment, and advantage. My reconstruction of Charles's practice suggests a lack of clarity on the part of both proprietor and borrower about the circulating library book's status during the loan period. Such libraries, therefore, could offer the impecunious borrower opportunities to use prestigious or in-demand books to strengthen affective ties within patronage networks and amatory relationships. However, ultimately the loan's liminal proprietorial status could also hamper their ability to use the book to its full potential effect. Charles's documented circulation of *Evelina* invites us to reconsider both the role of libraries in expanding the reading nation, and the ways in which they shaped readers' affective relations with texts.

Structure of the Element

This Element consists of five sections and an Afterword. Section 1 provides information about Charles's early life, which helps the reader to understand the nuances of his usage of *Evelina*. Drawing on his unpublished manuscript letters and poems, I highlight his interest in theatrical culture and the tension between his scholarly and creative ambitions. I also examine his adolescent relationship

---

[19] Certeau, *The Practice of Everyday Life*.

[20] Allan, *A Nation of Readers*; Towsey, *Reading the Scottish Enlightenment*; Fergus, *Provincial Readers;* Colclough, *Consuming Texts*: Mee and Sangster, 'Introduction'.

with Frances, emphasising an embryonic literary rivalry, which I locate within the well-documented desire among Burney siblings to please the family patriarch, Dr Charles Burney (1726–1814). Following his arrival in Aberdeen, I sketch the contours of Charles's social circles and activities over the three years he spent in Scotland. I draw particular attention to Charles's self-presentation as a young man of letters and his attempts to position himself as a suppliant for patronage, to women as well as men. Particularly important is his habit of circulating his own original manuscript poetry alongside (or within) printed texts selected to bear witness to his literary taste.

Section 2 reconstructs Charles's documented encounters with his sister's novel between 1777 and 1781. Noting his crucial role in helping Frances to preserve her anonymity with Lowndes in 1777, I build up a picture of his interactions with three separate sets of the published novel, which I call the Shinfield *Evelina*, the Aberdeen *Evelina*, and the Banff *Evelina*. Charles's engagement with the text is marked by three key features. First, he is an energetic participant in prescribed and informal loan economies. He draws on both the resources of local circulating libraries and personal favours to obtain sets of *Evelina*, before sub-lending them to other parties. Second, he displays an interactive style of engagement with the text in 'prefixing' a poem of his own composition and using marginalia to reference personal jokes. Finally, he shows a tendency to inhabit, perform, and project characters from the diegesis created by Frances, and to encourage similar responses in fellow readers.

Section 3 analyses the sonnet addressed to 'the Female Reader', which Charles reports 'prefix[ing]' to the Aberdeen *Evelina*. I evaluate Charles's sonnet as verse inscription, showing that it establishes a set of belletristic parameters within which 'the female reader' might respond to the novel and promotes the poet's own literary gifts alongside the novelist's.[21] I then consider it as a prefatory piece of paratext, which enables Charles to join his sister (the author) and his father (the dedicatee of the prefatory Ode) on the page.[22] This section, then, adds a further characteristic to Charles's reader profile: the tendency to superimpose his desired identity as belletrist over Frances's own as novelist.

Section 4 argues that Charles identified strongly with the character of the poor Scottish poet Mr Macartney, and that he 'performed' Macartney through his poetic and sociable practice. Here, I read Charles's manuscript poetry alongside the verses attributed to Macartney within *Evelina*. Charles's 'Verse Letter to FJHW', composed as he read *Evelina* for the first time, replicates the core tropes of Macartney's 'unfinished verses, beginning 'O LIFE!'. Similarly, his odes to

---

[21] Jackson, *Marginalia.* [22] Genette, *Paratexts;* Doody, *The Life in the Works.*

Nancy Gordon, Rachel Willox, and Jessy Willox, composed just as he was lending *Evelina* to these young women, bear marked similarities to Macartney's verses dropped in the pump room. Charles's correspondence suggests that he positioned himself as a gallant suppliant to the Willox sisters just as Macartney does to Evelina, and that he placed his relationship towards them along similar axes of brother/lover. Briefly, I also contextualise Charles's identified performances by considering other contemporary reader responses to Frances Burney's fiction from readers, including Queen Charlotte (1744–1818), Hannah More (1745–1833), Maria Edgeworth (1768–1849), and Jane Austen (1775–1817). Across this set of responses, I highlight consistent anxiety about the prospect of young female readers taking Frances Burney's characters as models and developing unrealistic aspirations or undesirable behaviours as a result. Ironically, Charles's identified performance of Macartney suggests that young men might have been more vulnerable to such a danger.

In the final section, Section 5, I consider Charles as a precarious agent within a loan economy centred around mass-produced print texts. I first examine him as a borrower, comparing his documented uses of the book to the prescriptive 'Conditions' of the library which may have lent it to him. I argue that the scale of Charles's subletting practice should provoke us to reconsider how one loan may have spawned many readers, with significant implications for the scale of readership during this period and the impact of libraries on the reading nation.[23] Moreover, I compare his tactile engagement with the Aberdeen and Banff *Evelina*s to his mutilation of the stolen Cambridge books a few years earlier, asking what such acts of defacement might suggest about how different libraries exerted various forms of proprietorship over their holdings.[24] I then consider him as a lender of the text, who uses it to solicit patronage and express amatory aspiration. In a case study tracking the affective character of Charles's sub-loans to the sisters Rachel and Jessy Willox, I evaluate his attempt to create a reading community in which demonstrations of his literary prowess alongside his sister's would be repaid by amatory and material advantage. More broadly, I suggest that, within scholarship around gift exchange, material culture, and the history of emotions, the loan as concept and practice deserves greater attention. In Charles Burney's cycle of lending and reclaiming his sister's novel, one can access a sense of his insecurity in sociable, literary, and economic spheres, and see how he attempted to exploit opportunities offered by print and manuscript cultures to bolster his own footing.[25]

---

[23] Allan, *A Nation of Readers*, 214.   [24] University of Cambridge Library, X.6.36 and X.12.28.
[25] Holloway, *The Game of Love*; Zionkowski and Klekar, *The Culture of the Gift*; Mauss, *The Gift*.

The Afterword synthesises my findings, concludes the narrative of Charles's time in Scotland, and provides a brief overview of the rest of his life. I highlight his ambivalent role in his famous sister's literary career; he promoted and embellished her fictional and dramatic productions to the extent that, from the 1790s, she consistently referred to him as 'her dear Agent'.[26] I draw attention to the many surviving sources which might shed light on his life and works, including his approximately 2,500 unpublished letters and poems, and his vast collections in the British Library. I frame him as a fascinating figure for whom textuality and sociability were paradigmatically linked, whose singular 'Mad Rage for Possessing a Library' (as Frances termed it) has the potential to help us rewrite the history of Romantic bibliomania.[27] Finally, I reflect on the methodologies used to piece together the story of *Evelina* in Scotland, highlighting the thriving interdisciplinary field of Burney Studies as a site where such methodologies can work together to great effect.

1 Introducing Charles Burney

Charles Burney was born in King's Lynn, Norfolk, on 4 December 1757.[28] He was the fifth living child of Charles Burney (1726–1814), organist and music teacher, and Esther Burney (née Sleepe, 1725–62), proprietor of a fan shop in Cheapside.[29] When Charles was four, the Burneys moved from Norfolk to London, taking a house in Poland Street.[30] During Charles's childhood and adolescence, this household was lively and cultured, despite the family being far from wealthy. During the 1760s and 1770s, the senior Charles Burney was networking furiously and travelling extensively – alongside a busy teaching schedule – in an attempt to consolidate his reputation as Britain's foremost historian of music.[31] As a result, his children frequently received visits from celebrities of the day, most notably David Garrick, who would visit with his spaniel Phil and stage impromptu performances for the children.[32]

Frances records that Charles was a great admirer of Garrick, who nicknamed his young fan 'Cherry-Nose … on account of his nose being rather of the brightest,' and that the little boy would 'smirk and simper' when favoured with his idol's attention.[33] Charles's own writings also testify that these visits made a considerable impression. When Garrick died, the twenty-two-year-old

---

[26] Frances Burney D'Arblay and Alexandre D'Arblay to Charles Burney, 17 June 1796, *JL* 3:168.
[27] Frances Burney to Charles Parr Burney, 26 February 1818, *JL* 10:795.
[28] Scholes, *The Great Dr Burney*, 1:84.   [29] Erickson, 'Esther Sleepe'.
[30] Hemlow, *History*, Ch. 1-2.   [31] Sabor, 'The March of Intimacy'.   [32] Hemlow, *History*, 13.
[33] Frances Burney, Journal for 1775, *EJL* 1:96.

Charles penned passionate elegies mourning his genius.[34] And shortly before his own death at the age of sixty, as the proud owner of a 'collection of Prints and Drawings of [Garrick] … not to be matched', Charles would write: 'scarcely a [day] passes in which the memory of Mr Garrick does not recur to my recollection'.[35]

1.1 Charterhouse

Charles entered Charterhouse School on 15 February 1768 at the age of ten and departed on 10 April 1777 aged nineteen.[36] He boarded during term time but returned home to London during the holidays. In September 1768, Frances notes in her journal, 'My sweet [baby] Charles is come home – he is well, hearty, & full of spirits, mirth & good-humour. My Aunt Nanny who went lately to see him at the Charter House, was assured there that he was the sweetest temper'd Boy in the school.'[37]

It is around this time that Charles's own archive begins. A handful of letters and poems survive from his time at Charterhouse – mostly addressed to Frances, to whom he was apparently close. Some of these describe Charles's studies and academic progress, foreshadowing the scholarly application that would eventually make him one of the leading classicists of the early Romantic period. Aged eleven, he informs Frances that 'all our Form are fagging at turner very hard'.[38] Aged twelve, he copies out a Greek alphabet for her – 'I am sure you will be Charmed with it … there is a great number of odd letter's but you are so well aquainted with the Language that I need not tell you that' [sic] – and spells her name in Greek characters, apologising for the lack of a letter corresponding to 'F'.[39] But elsewhere he hints that such application might not come entirely naturally. He does 'fag hard in search of further knowledge' but there is a good reason for such diligent application: 'Berdmore is really very strict, / And will sharp punishment inflict, / Of idleness – & therefore I / Wholly to Greek my mind apply.'[40]

In fact, the teenage Charles evidently had a range of interests, the most apparent of which is his poetic inclination. He often composes light verse to entertain – or tease – friends and family. In a poem dated 3 May 1774, Frances is accused of 'flirting about town', while a braggart school friend is advised:

---

[34] 'Garrick', Osborn c37 62–3; 'Ode, to the Memory of David Garrick', Osborn c35, 57–8. Throughout the Element, manuscript poems are sometimes referenced with a shortened title.
[35] Charles Burney to Frances Burney, 18 September 1817, Berg 196370B.
[36] Scholes, *The Great Dr Burney*, 1:344–345.   [37] Frances Burney, Journal 1768, *EJL* 1:33.
[38] Charles Burney to Frances Burney, 13 December 1768, OSB MSS 3, Box 6, Folder 379.
[39] Charles Burney to Frances Burney, 11 October 1769, OSB MSS 3, Box 6, Folder 379.
[40] Charles Burney to Frances Burney, 3 May 1774, OSB MSS 3, Box 6, Folder 379. Samuel Berdmore (1739–1802) was master of Charterhouse School 1769–90.

If you should meet a matchless Dame,
Whom youth & beauty grace,
Before you hope to gain her heart
Pray hide your ugly face.[41]

Frances Burney could evidently give as good as she got, since one of Charles's letters indicates that his nose had recently been a subject of ribaldry: 'Indeed Madam I don't like your severe Sarcasm upon my Poor Nose [... which] to be sure has little of the Redish Cast.'[42] Despite such badinage, he clearly missed his family immensely when at school. He eagerly enquires after various members, declares that he 'long[s] to ... come home', and on one occasion remarks plaintively, 'I thought you had almost forgot Carlo Dolci.'[43] When he did return for the holidays he deployed his poetic knack for the amusement of his siblings, as in an 'Occasional Prologue' to Goldsmith's *The Good Natur'd Man*, intended to be delivered following a domestic performance by the Burney children.[44] His passion for theatre is evident in several of these items – for example, a long verse-letter in which he enviously imagines Frances visiting theatres and concerts in London and enjoying performances by Garrick and Jane Barsanti.[45]

1.2 Cambridge

Charles departed Charterhouse on 10 April 1777, bound for Caius College at the University of Cambridge.[46] He had been studying there for only a few months when his theft was discovered in late October, and he was promptly expelled.[47] The principal contemporary account of the crime, written by the antiquary William Cole, describes Charles as a 'very studious & industrious' student. 'Insomuch, that he was admitted into the Public [University] Library, tho' an Undergraduate' and 'regularly came every Day & stayed till the Doors were closed'. A certain 'Marshall the Schole Keeper' began to observe that 'a great Number [of books] had been taken away, chiefly classical Books of Elzevir Editions'.

> [H]e began to suspect Mr Berney, & complained to Mr. Whisson, the Under Librarian, who advised him to be quiet, & contrive to get into his Chambers, & see if he could discover any of the lost Books: the Bedmaker

[41] 'Extempore on Jullian's ... ', Osborn c37, 67.
[42] Charles Burney to Frances Burney, undated, OSB MSS 3, Box 6, Folder 379.
[43] Charles Burney to Frances Burney, 11 October 1769 and undated, both in OSB MSS 3, Box 6, Folder 379.
[44] 'Occasional Prologue', Osborn c37, 40–42.
[45] Charles Burney to Frances Burney, undated, OSB MSS 3, Box 6, Folder 379.
[46] Scholes, *The Great Dr Burney*, 1:344–345.
[47] For a full account of his time at Cambridge and its consequences, see Walker, 'Charles Burney's Theft'.

said, it would be difficult, as her Master was very studious, & hardly ever 20 Minutes out of his Room at a time except at Dinner Time: he got in at that Time & found about 35 Classical Books in a dark Corner, which he had taken the University Arms out of, & put his own in their place; & the Tutor being spoken to, he went into Hall the Day it was first discovered to him & then disappeared: & this Week a Box of Books belonging to the Library was sent from London, whither he had sent them. What further will be done is unknown. I pity his Father, who must sensibly feel the Stroke; as the young Man can never appear again in the University & so his views in this way utterly overturned.[48]

Dr Burney did indeed 'sensibly feel the Stroke'. As Walker notes, he was incensed at his son's crime and considered disowning him. For the present, there was no possibility of Charles returning to the family home. He was sent to the village of Shinfield in Berkshire, where he would remain until gossip died down and a decision could be made about his future.

1.3 Shinfield

Although Charles lived in Shinfield for almost a year, Walker provides little information about his life there, blaming the paltry archive. He remarks only that Charles 'felt decidedly superior to the rustic circle in which he found himself', citing his poetical satire on 'such features of Shinfield life as the preaching of the little Welsh curate, the jangling of the Church bell, and the inharmonious singing of the village choir'.[49] This summary does not do full justice to Charles's carefully curated archive of verse dating from 1778. Numerous affectionate poems dedicated to members of Shinfield society survive, which cumulatively show him flexing his sociable and literary muscles during this period, using verse to cement and commemorate key relationships.[50]

This verse also provides valuable biographical information. For example, it has long been a mystery to Burney scholars why Shinfield was chosen as the place for Charles's exile, or who cared for him while he lived there.[51] The poetry suggests a probable answer. Upon his departure from Shinfield in 1778, Charles writes parting verses for four members of the Francis family: 'Mr Francis',

---

[48] William Cole, *Collections for an Athenae Cantabrigienses, d*. BM Add. MS. 5864, p. 318. Qtd in Walker, 'Charles Burney's Theft', 314. See Section 5 for more detailed discussion of Charles's motives and mutilation practice.

[49] Walker, 'Charles Burney's Theft', 314–315. Here Walker refers to 'On the Bells at Shinfield Church', Osborn c37, 39; 'Epigrams on the Shinfield Singers', Osborn c37, 56; and 'On Mr Jane – Curate of Shinfield', Osborn c37, 56.

[50] See 'On the death of Peter Floyer', Osborn c37, 37; 'To Mr Grantham', Osborn c37, 13–16; and 'To Mr Badger', Osborn c37, 12–13.

[51] See Walker, 'Charles Burney's Theft', 314–315, and *EJL* 3:13, n. 26.

'Master William Francis', 'Miss Polly Francis', and 'Master James Francis'.[52]
It seems that the Master of Shinfield School around 1780 was one William
Francis, a mathematician who appears as a correspondent in the pages of several
literary and scientific periodicals.[53] The *Pedigree Register* confirms his occupation and location in 1778, and the name of his eldest son.[54] Given Francis's
pedagogical qualifications, Charles's familiar relationship with his children, and
a reference to Mrs Francis in one of his letters (see Section 2), I think it probable
that following his Cambridge disgrace Charles was entrusted to the care of the
Francis family.[55] In any event, by the time he left Shinfield, he was reminiscing
over happy days spent there swimming in the river and playing card games,
sentimentally characterising the village as the home of 'peace', 'endless loves',
and 'social mirth'.[56]

During the Shinfield period, Charles's poems and letters also record intensive
engagement with news and periodical print culture, both local and metropolitan.
Possibly imitating or encouraged by William Francis, he pens poetic answers to
enigmas in the *Gentleman's Diary* and *Ladies' Diary*.[57] He participates in
a topical debate raging within the pages of the *Reading Mercury* (to which
Francis also contributed poetry), versifying in defence of a surgeon called
Cundall who promoted the controversial practice of inoculation.[58] He also
composes verses on recent London scandals, indicating that he had access to
such gossip either via correspondence or the newspapers.[59] Some of these
poems, like those written at Charterhouse, are doggerel or light verse clearly
designed to amuse. But Charles also begins to attempt, during the year 1779,
a neoclassical poetic diction. His poetry starts to address topics such as friendship, virtue, and the callousness of fate, using a register characterised by
archaism, epithet, abstraction, and periphrasis. These shifts in form and tone
may demonstrate the growing influence of Charles's classical knowledge on his
poetic development, or a more serious outlook on life following the

---

[52] 'To Mr Francis', Osborn c37, 8; 'To Master William Francis', Osborn c37, 17; 'To Miss Polly
Francis', Osborn c37, 17–19; 'To Master James Francis', Osborn c37, 19–21.
[53] Francis submitted answers to the 'mathematical correspondence' section in *The London
Magazine, or Gentleman's Monthly Intelligencer*, 1775, 417 and 1779, 34. He can also be
found providing answers to an enigma in *The Ladies' Diary*, 1780, 16.
[54] Sherwood, *The Pedigree Register*, 166–168.
[55] Undated and unattributed fragment labelled 'Note on Evelina in unknown hand, post 1777', OSB
MSS 3 Box 5 f. 346. See below and Section 2 for my attribution to Charles.
[56] 'A Farewell to Shinfield', Osborn c37, 9–11.
[57] 'Answer to the Prize Enigma, Osborn c37, 24; 'Answer to all the Enigmas', Osborn c37, 25–27.
[58] *Reading Mercury*, 23 July 1781, qtd in Sherwood, *The Pedigree Register*, 168. 'Parody on some
lines signed Fidelia' and 'To Mr Cundal' are both in Osborn c37, 28–29.
[59] 'On the quarrels of the Pantheon Committee', Osborn c37, 22–3; and 'On the Quarrels of the
Pantheon Committee', Osborn c35, 27–28.

consequences of his theft. In Section 4, I argue that they are also influenced by the signature style(s) of Frances Burney's poet Macartney in *Evelina*.

During the Shinfield period, Frances Burney is Charles's only known correspondent. In a journal entry for 30 March 1778, she remarks, 'I have just received a Letter from poor Charles, in which he informs me that he has subscribed to a Circulating Library at Reading – & then he adds, "I am to have *Evelina* to Day; the man told me that it was spoken very highly of."'[60] Unfortunately, none of Frances's own correspondence to Charles from the period survives. However, two fragmentary letters from him to her, of which Walker was apparently unaware, do.[61] Although undated, they must have been written after Frances's mention of the Reading circulating library at the end of March 1778, but before Charles left Shinfield in October. These two fragments are notable first because they contain Charles's first recorded response to *Evelina* (see Section 2), and second because one of them suggests that during his time in Shinfield Charles was helping Frances to improve her Latin. He corrects her translation of a passage of Seneca, which she had apparently sent him in a previous letter.[62] It is tempting to read this letter, alongside Charles's 1769 reference to Frances's interest in Greek, as two points in a long-standing adolescent exchange about classical languages and literatures.

The implications of this possibility are twofold. The first concerns Frances Burney's access to stereotypically masculine forms of knowledge. It is well-known that she briefly studied Latin in her late twenties – an accomplishment often deemed risky for a woman, since it might indicate a desire to transgress gendered spheres of learning and aspire to 'bluestocking' fame. However, this has usually been presented as an honour thrust upon her by Dr Johnson, which was only pursued for a short period before her father persuaded her to return to more traditionally feminine literary activities. Burney herself has been understood – based on her own letters to her sister Susan – as a reluctant scholar who feared the implications of being known to study the classics and lamented 'devot[ing] so much Time to acquire something I shall always dread to have known'.[63] But these previously unremarked letters between Charles and Frances suggest that she was willingly studying Latin a full year before

---

[60] Frances Burney, Journal 1778, 30 March, *EJL* 3:13.

[61] The first ('Saturday morning', undated, OSB MSS 3, Box 6, Folder 379) has been attributed to Charles in the Beinecke's catalogue. The second ('Note on Evelina in unknown hand', OSB MSS 3, Box 5 f. 346) is unattributed. I am confident that it is Charles's hand, and internal evidence suggests strongly that he is the author: see Section 2.

[62] The letter containing Frances's translation has not survived. However, the timing would be broadly synonymous with Johnson's attempt to teach her Latin. See Justice, *Manufacturers of Literature*, 195. See also *EJL* 3:336.

[63] Justice, *Manufacturers of Literature*, 195; *EJL* 3:336.

Johnson offered to teach her, indicating that she was more eager than she would admit to acquire classical learning. The second implication concerns the routes by which Frances Burney accessed specialist knowledge and intellectual fulfilment during the early years of her literary career. The Streatham environment dominated by Johnson is often pinpointed as crucial in this respect. But it may be that in focusing so heavily on his influence, and that of Hester Thrale, we have neglected to see what was available to Frances within her family unit. Despite his disgrace and exile, her 'sweet [baby] Charles' – who of course had benefited from the first-class education she could never have had – was supporting her intellectual development just as actively as, and long before, Johnson.

However, it is important not to overstate Charles's generosity in assuming a pedagogical relationship towards his celebrated sister, since it probably conveyed a form of gratification that was far from selfless. In the 1778 letter discussing *Evelina* and Seneca, it is striking how little space Charles devotes to celebrating Frances's recent literary achievement (two lines) in comparison to correcting her faulty Latin (more than forty). In doing so, his tone is in places rather patronising, offering backhanded compliments such as 'your emendations *in general* please me' and scolding her for contracting verbs: 'It cannot be *confin'd*: for *fin* does not spell *fine* – & so in the other Verbs of this sort.' Overall, the tone and content of the letter subordinates Frances's creative achievement to Charles's own critical expertise. This was not the last time he would attempt to assert himself in such a manner.

By autumn of 1778, the next step in Charles's career was determined: Dr Burney and his friends decided that the black sheep of the family should finish his education at King's College, Aberdeen.[64] 'Let me shake off the rustic', Charles declares in his final Shinfield poem, '& once more / The gayer joys of College life explore'.[65] He made the long journey northward between October and the end of that year, and was settled in Aberdeen by the beginning of 1779.[66]

1.4 Aberdeen and Banff

Charles's archive contains no material describing the journey from Shinfield to Aberdeen. Neither does it address his arrival in the city or his living quarters. However, plenty of information exists in the published memoirs of two of his contemporaries: the playwright George Colman (1762–1836), who attended King's College between 1781 and 1783, and the abolitionist James Stephen

---

[64] Walker, 'Charles Burney's Theft', 315; Scholes, *The Great Dr Burney,* 1:347.
[65] 'A Farewell to Shinfield', Osborn c37, 9–11. [66] *EJL* 3:193, n. 83.

(1758–1832), who attended Marischal College between 1775 and 1778.[67] Both, like Charles, had previously been Londoners, and they offer scathing accounts of their new home: a town resembling 'a long dreary village' which was 'very unsightly and mean to an eye accustomed to London'.[68] Colman, who lived in the same building as Burney, is contemptuous about his 'small sitting-room' and second-hand furniture, but mollified by the fact that at least his quarters are the envy of his Scottish peers at King's, 'young barbarians, migrating from their mountains, to be half-civilised'.[69] He is also dismissive of the College's attempt to impose academic rigour, noting that during the short five-month term there was 'no discipline at all'. Although he did not apparently dislike his tutors, he makes it clear that they did not exercise any authority over the students,[70] and recalls learning by solitary study, borrowing books from the college library and poring over them in his rooms. He reports hearing from mutual friends that Charles Burney, during his time at King's, had done likewise, shut away in his chambers 'unaided by Scottish professors [and] secluding himself like a hermit'.[71]

However, as Colman's editor Richard Brinsley Peake notes, this character-isation of Charles as a studious 'hermit' should be taken with a pinch of salt.[72] In fact, if we turn to his extant letters and verses, which recommence from February 1779, it is clear that he enjoyed a lively social life in Aberdeen. Though he writes to Frances, in a vein of snobbery similar to Colman's, that 'in aspect, appearance, & dress, [his fellow students] look marvelously like plough boys' [sic], he takes care to note 'a few exceptions' where 'a natural good breeding, acquired by narrow observation, guided by a solid understand-ing, has been able to shake off *highland rust*'.[73] As I show in Figure 1, such Aberdeen friends as James Gray (1761–94), Robert Burnside (1759–1826), Abercrombie Gordon (1758–1821), and Gilbert Gerard (1760–1815) provide some of the most extensive, vivid, and informative letters in Charles's Scottish archive.[74]

Recalling Colman's observation that King's tutors did not stand on ceremony with their students, it seems that Charles was also friendly with his tutors: James Dunbar (1742–98, Professor of Moral Philosophy), Thomas Gordon (1714–97, Professor of Philosophy), and Alexander Gerard (1728–95, Professor of Divinity). In summary, Charles was taking his place in a small community,

---

[67] Peake, *Memoirs*, vol.2; Stephen, *Memoirs*.   [68] Peake, *Memoirs*, 85; Stephen, *Memoirs*, 176.
[69] Peake, *Memoirs*, 83, 81.   [70] Peake, *Memoirs*, 89–90.   [71] Peake, *Memoirs*, 88, 84.
[72] Peake adds a footnote explaining that Charles was in fact a "bon vivant" (2:84).
[73] Charles Burney to Frances Burney, [1780], OSB MSS 3, Box 6, Folder 427.
[74] For example, Burnside describes a hair-raising encounter with a press gang on a sea voyage from Aberdeen to London, while Gray makes a fine art of teasing Charles about his love affairs.

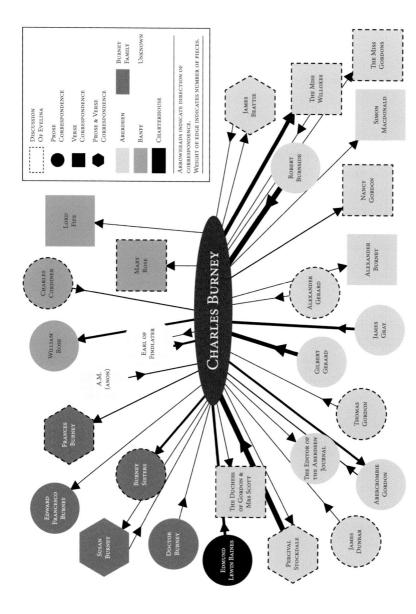

Figure 1 Visualisation of Charles Burney's correspondence network from January 1779 to August 1781. Designed by Sophie Coulombeau and Rich Hardiman.

where academic, social, and domestic spheres frequently overlapped. Charles befriended the sons of his tutors and flirted with their daughters. He was invited to their town houses during the term and stayed at their estates during the vacation. Through them he also met other members of Aberdeen gentry such as the Burnet and Willox families.

Rachel and Jessy Willox, whom I address in Section 5, merit a special mention. As well as in Charles's own letters and poetry, we can find biographical information about them in the family memoir of the Dingwall Fordyce family (into which Rachel eventually married) and James Stephen's *Memoirs*.[75] Stephen, who knew the sisters personally, describes the Miss Willoxes as 'the most celebrated beauties of the place ... in whose education [their father, the Baillie of Aberdeen George Willox] had spared no cost, so that they were as much distinguished by their accomplishments as by their beauty'. He also notes their mother's eagerness to 'assist them in finding advantageous settlements in marriage ... Every young man of fortune or good expectations in life found easy access to them under the parental roof'. Stephen characterises Rachel as 'the finest and most graceful figure I ever saw', with 'the best complexion', 'a profusion of flaxen hair', 'large blue eyes [with] great expression and power', and features expressing 'dignity'. He describes Jessy as 'also very handsome... [some] thought her more so than her Sister, tho' much inferior to her in understanding'.[76] Stephen's descriptions accord closely with Charles's own account of the sisters, which we find in a letter to Frances, highlighting the 'agreeable ... liveliness' of 'the lovely' Jessy's temper, while praising the 'milder graces' and 'conscious dignity' of Rachel's. Interestingly, he uses Samuel Richardson's novel *Sir Charles Grandison* (1754) to gloss them further: 'Jessy is a Charlotte G, and Rachel, what Lady L, might have been before marriage – You remember *Sir Cha. Grandison*. *Love* would be the *food* of Rachel's life, & the *seasoning* of Jessy's!'[77] Charlotte Grandison, of course, is presented in Richardson's novel as 'frank, easy and good-humoured' with 'a vein of raillery, that were she not polite, would give one too much apprehension for one's ease', whereas Lady L has 'true female softness and delicacy', with 'so much sweetness and complacency, that you are not so much afraid of her as you are of her sister'.[78]

Throughout the early spring of 1779, Charles doles out his poetic compliments equally to several young ladies, but by May he had clearly become

[75] Rachel Willox (d. 1789) and Janet "Jessy" Willox (d. 1788). Dingwall Fordyce, *Family Record*, 248–249 and xc–xci.
[76] Stephen, *Memoirs,* 190–195.
[77] Charles Burney to Frances Burney, [Feb/ March 1780], OSB MSS 3, Box 6, Folder 427.
[78] Richardson, *Charles Grandison*, 1:258-9, 1:306.

infatuated with 'my adorable Jessy'. In the letter to Frances containing his account of *Evelina*'s reception, he praises Jessy's 'liveliness, sweetness & goodness', making much of his 'affection' for her even though he considered his 'unsettled state' a prohibition to 'speaking out'.[79] He also writes a poem praising her 'beauties' and swearing that time will only 'improve' his passion.[80] It is not clear whether his affection was returned. During 1779, his friends seem to have considered him 'a settled man', but he also laments Jessy's occasional 'coldness' and expresses anxiety that she does not 'burn with the same flame' as he does.[81] Charles was also clearly friendly with Rachel, since he writes her a long poem to celebrate her 'recovery from a dangerous illness', and four of his poems address the two young women collectively. His intense interest in the sisters is evident until the late summer of 1780, when Jessy abruptly (and, for Charles, unexpectedly) married another suitor.[82]

Charles was not in Aberdeen when Jessy's engagement took place, because – like many of his peers – he spent his long vacations travelling the north-east of Scotland. The trip he took in the summer of 1780 – upon which he took a set of *Evelina* with him – is particularly well-evidenced, since he kept a detailed travel journal, intended for his sisters.[83] He spent significant time in Banffshire, for part of which he was the guest of James Duff, 2nd Earl of Fife (1729–1809), and became acquainted with Fife's factor William Rose (1740–1807), Rose's wife Mary (1757–1838), and the Banff minister Charles Cordiner (1746–94). As mentioned in Section 3, he developed a passionate crush on Mary Rose and left *Evelina* in her custody when he returned from Banff to Aberdeen in the autumn of 1780.

During Charles's final year of study, his archive becomes sparser. A rare letter remarks, 'the College is very full this year but it might as well be empty for me – as there is not one whom I ever speak to, or see in my rooms'. However, he was not bereft of entertainment: 'the Players are in town' and 'I go every night; except when I am otherwise particularly engaged'.[84] It is likely – though Charles does not mention it – that he was gambling heavily during this time, given the parlous state of his finances which emerged later in the year. His impending graduation, and the question mark remaining over his future, seem to

---

[79] Charles Burney to Frances Burney, [May/June 1779], OSB MSS 3, Box 6, Folder 381.
[80] 'To Miss J. Willox', Osborn c37, unpaginated.
[81] Gilbert Gerard to Charles Burney, [1778/9?], OSB MSS 3, Box 9, Folder 704; Charles Burney to Frances Burney [May–June 1779], OSB MSS 3, Box 6, Folder 381; Robert Burnside to Charles Burney, 30 June 1779, OSB MSS 3, Box 3, Folder 158.
[82] Captain John Campbell of the 72nd Regiment (d.1796.)
[83] Charles Burney, Journal-letter to his sister, Susan Elizabeth (Burney) Phillips, 1780, OSB MSS 3 Box 7, Folder 442. See also Walker, 'Charles Burney's Tour'.
[84] Charles Burney to Abercrombie Gordon, 20 January 1781, OSB MSS 3, Box 7, Folder 337.

have been weighing on his mind, since he asks several friends whether they can help him obtain a curacy, without any success.[85]

Between September 1780 and January 1781, Charles became acquainted with James Ogilvy, Earl of Seafield and Findlater (1750–1811), an important figure in queer history. Though married, Findlater was well known to prefer men to women; he lived the last two decades of his life, and eventually shared a grave, with his partner Johann Fischer.[86] The nature of the relationship between Findlater and Charles during the early 1780s is unclear, but surviving correspondence between them suggests a certain intimacy. In January 1781, in a letter which he warns Charles is 'not meant for publication', Findlater praises Charles's 'Attractions' and describes the 'Friendship' between them as 'founded by Reason & … fostered by Passion … When will you leave your Doctors & Diplomas to come to me?' He also jokes about his wife's dislike of Charles: she 'hates whoever I am attached to, with a Uniformity that does Honour to her Perseverance, if not her Heart'.[87] The correspondence indicates that Findlater offered Charles significant financial support during his final months in Aberdeen. In April 1781, he agrees to send Charles thirty guineas, which he hopes will 'be sufficient for the Expense of the *Menus Plaisirs* of last Winter'.[88]

Findlater also seems to have offered to take Charles on an imminent trip to London, and en route to introduce him to the Archbishop of York with a view to easing his path to ordination. Charles apparently reported this prospect to his father with some excitement, but Dr Burney's response sounds a note of caution and suggests that he was pretty alert to the nature of Findlater's attachment to his son:

> None are treated in such a Manner as you have been, by several great Personages in Scotland, but for something wch they are pleased to admit as an equivalent – Pure Friendship is imagined to be the most disinterested of all affections; but I fear when accurately examined it will turn out to be as selfish as many other Passions of a grosser Name … as to Ld Fin–ter's affection for you it seems like that of David for Jonathan, so 'wonderful as to suggest the Love of Woman' … You have never yet mentioned L^y F--------ter – is my L^d a Married Man? Has he Children?[89]

---

[85] Edmund Lewin Baines to Charles Burney, 4 August 1781, OSB MSS 3, Box 2, Folder 82; Percival Stockdale to Charles Burney, 4 June 1781, Osborn c6.

[86] For Findlater's sexuality, see: *EJL* 4:418, n. 78; Harvey, *Sex in Georgian England*, 2001, 137; Nedobity 2007; Päckert and Klyne, *Lord Findlater und die Gärten seiner Zeit*, 2022.

[87] James Ogilvy to Charles Burney, 17 January 1781, OSB MSS 3, Box 13, Folder 997.

[88] James Ogilvy to Charles Burney, 13 April 1781, OSB MSS 3, Box 13, Folder 997. 'Menus Plaisirs' translates as 'small pleasures'.

[89] Dr Charles Burney to Charles Burney, 25 February 1781, *LCB* 1:316–22.

In the end, the trip never took place since Findlater withdrew his offer, citing his wife's objections to Charles as a travelling companion.[90] In April, the Findlaters set out for York and London, while Charles graduated in Aberdeen.[91]

Immediately after graduation, Charles was supposed to return to his family, but instead he lingered in Scotland for almost three months. In letters to his sisters written over the early summer, he declares that he cannot tear himself away from a new love interest called Jane Abernethie, a cousin of Lord Fife's: 'The Abernethie has so engrossed my affections, of late, that I lived, breathed, saw, heard, for her alone.'[92] This rather abrupt attachment is not evidenced by any amatory poetry like that produced for Jessy Willox or Mary Rose. Neither does Jane Abernethie appear to have been keen on Charles, since, by his own admission, she had forbidden him from writing to her. Nonetheless, when the Abernethie family moved from Aberdeen to Banff for the summer, Charles apparently followed them. Betty Rizzo suggests, very credibly, that the attachment was pragmatic rather than heartfelt, and that Charles hoped to persuade the well-born Abernethie to elope with him so he could secure a settlement to pay off his debts.[93] But such a plan, if it existed, appears to have come to nothing. The object of his intentions eventually took refuge with a remote aunt, and Charles finally began his overdue journey back to London. He arrived at St Martin's Street in the last week of July 1781. Bizarrely, he had brought with him a dog called Chloe, which he claimed that Jane Abernethie had given him, and which promptly gave birth to puppies.[94]

1.5 A Common Theme: Prospects, Poetry, and Patronage

Despite his Cambridge disgrace, and its implication that Charles took a somewhat cavalier approach to the Commandments, Dr Burney had nonetheless afterwards decided that he should complete his expensive education and pursue a career in the Anglican Church. As William Jacob notes, the office of clergyman was one of the three main professions pursued by intellectually gifted young men of the 'middling sort': it had a well-established practical framework for career advancement which could, if combined with a talent for

---

[90] James Ogilvy to Charles Burney, 16 March 1781, OSB MSS 3, Box 13, Folder 997.

[91] Many questions about the relationship between James Ogilvy and Charles Burney remain unanswered. I am grateful to Martin Päckert, Frank Klyne, and Wolfgang Nedobity for conversations on this topic.

[92] Charles Burney to Frances, Susanna, and Charlotte Burney, 21 May 1781, OSB MSS 3, Box 6, Folder 387.

[93] *EJL* 4:379, n. 6. As Charles's August correspondence with Findlater shows, he was in at least fifty pounds' worth of debt.

[94] Frances Burney to Hester Lynch Thrale, 29 July 1781, *EJL* 4:420.

generating patronage, take one to significant career heights.[95] Impeccably respectable, and with significant opportunities for academic honours and learned publication, it segued nicely with Dr Burney's aspirations for his most academically precocious child. Practically speaking, ordination candidates were expected to be fluent in Latin and Greek as well as to have sound theological understanding. Although there is evidence of regional variation, it is safe to say that most were university graduates.[96]

The primary purpose of the theology degree Charles was undertaking at Aberdeen was, therefore, to complete the education that had been cut short at Cambridge. The second, but hardly less important, objective was to establish and maintain an excellent character in the eyes of his tutors and other influential people. Dr Burney was explicit on this point when he wrote to his son in February 1781. Charles's priorities should be to 'pursue your Studies with diligence' and to 'quit the place with credit & propriety'. These two objectives would feed towards the next steps of obtaining a curacy (a training post, also sometimes called a 'title'), securing strong character references, and preparing for the 'important business' of ordination.[97]

Charles himself, however, was ambivalent about the path his father had prescribed for him. Correspondence from his friend Robert Burnside, already ordained, indicates that Charles had expressed 'tremors' about ordination, occasioning some gentle reproval: "If you remember, I asked you the last time I enjoyed the pleasure of your conversation what was your opinion concerning … the ends which a man of sense, of honesty, & worth ought to have in view in entering upon the ministerial function, &c. You replied you had not thought about these matters. Excuse me, if I think that the present time seems to me to be a very proper one for you to investigate these points".[98] Percival Stockdale, also ordained, writes a little more stiffly: 'I hope you will now employ yourself strenuously on *this* study, and look on your Profession as the noblest of all human professions, not-withstanding the superficial Ridicule; XXX and the despicable contempt of your most despicable contemporaries.'[99]

With such ambivalence about Charles's own prospects in mind, I want to consider the relationship between form and purpose in his poetic output during his Scottish years. I noted in my discussion of the Charterhouse and Shinfield poetry that Charles often dedicates his verses to individuals, either to mark a particular occasion or to praise the dedicatee. His Scottish poetry continues this tendency, but

---

[95] Jacob, *The Clerical Profession*, 39.   [96] Jacob, *The Clerical Profession*, 34, 44.

[97] Dr Charles Burney to Charles Burney, 25 February 1781, *LCB* 1: 316–322; Jacob, *The Clerical Profession*, 61.

[98] Robert Burnside to Charles Burney, 27 August 1781, OSB MSS 3, Box 3, Folder 158.

[99] Percival Stockdale to Charles Burney, 4 June 1781, Osborn c6.

combines it with a tendency to lament the poet's hard lot in life and promote his own literary gifts. His 'Ode Addressed to Alexander Burnet of Seaton House', for example, implores the fourth Laird of Kemnay and recently retired diplomat (1735–1802) to 'extend [his] fond esteem' to 'cheer the Bard', who contemplates an uncertain future. At risk of having his 'Bark ... tost' by 'storms', Charles is positioned as a humble suppliant for Burnet's favour, with only poetic gifts to offer in return. If they were only equal to the excellence of their subject, he grovels, they might 'with a fire immortal glow', and 'flourish ... with deathless garlands drest'. Similarly, in Charles's fragmentary ode addressed to Fife, he positions himself as the 'Bard' and 'laurel'd Poet' offering his patron a 'deathless song'.[100] His poetic address to James Beattie (1735–1803) unfolds along similar lines, declaring a desire to 'court thy smile' by 'sing[ing Beattie's] praise'.[101]

The recurrent suppliant poetic positioning suggests that these verses can be read as emphatic, if indistinct, solicitations for patronage. Scholars of eighteenth-century patronage have long recognised the crucial role performed by poetry in soliciting and securing support from patrons. Moreover, in recent decades, they have broadened their understanding of the forms that literary patronage might take beyond the relatively narrow confines of hard cash or lucrative posts.[102] A more expansive set of categories – hospitality, material gifts, approbation, endorsements, advice, and introductions (to spaces or individuals) – is now recognised as crucial to the ways in which authors burnished their reputations and built earning power.[103] Charles might have been soliciting any of these forms of patronage when he set out using his poetry to 'widen the circle of his acquaintance'.[104] We have seen one example, in his correspondence with Findlater, of the tangible benefits that he hoped to obtain from friendships with eminent men. Such endeavours stood upon the foundation of flattery and self-promotion evidenced by his verse.

Crucially, however, the dedicatees are oddly placed to help Charles further the aims that Dr Burney had instructed him to pursue. Of the twelve people for whom epistolary poetry survives, five are marriageable young ladies and two are older women (see Figure 1). Of the remaining five, Fife is a politician (who only had Episcopalian livings in his gift, and whom Dr Burney did not consider likely to offer meaningful patronage);[105] Alexander Burnet is a former

---

[100] 'Fragment: Then was the towering Arch uprear'd ... '. Osborn c35, 70–71.
[101] 'Elegy, addressed to Dr Beattie', Osborn c35, 43–46.
[102] Griffin, *Literary Patronage*, 18–29.
[103] Eger, 'The Bluestocking Circle', in Eger and Peltz, *Brilliant Women*, 43.
[104] Robert Burnside to Charles Burney, 31 May 1779, OSB MSS 3, Box 3, Folder 158.
[105] In a letter of 11 September 1780, Abercombie Gordon tells Charles, 'if you could think of becoming a Presbyterian Clergyman Lord Fife has it in his power to provide *very handsomely for you*'. OSB MSS 3, Box 10, Folder 717.

diplomat, James Beattie is a poet and an essayist, and Simon Macdonald is an ensign in the navy.[106] The only clergyman to whom Charles dedicates poetry, Percival Stockdale, was notoriously bad at the job, and poorly placed to help Charles develop a career in the Church.[107] There is no evidence that Charles dedicated poetry to any of his tutors, or to senior clergy who might be able to help him find a title. The poems are just as poorly targeted in terms of composition as circulation, since they are overwhelmingly occasional, secular, and vernacular. The odd Latin epigraph aside, they make little attempt to showcase Charles's classical or theological learning.

Charles's verses dedicated to women require separate consideration, since they reproduce the suppliant positioning of those addressed to Beattie, Fife, and Burnet, but with a gendered twist. He begs the Willox sisters, for example, to treat him as a pet, who might '[a]ttend your toilets – set your caps – / Or rest, thrice happy, in your laps. / Make me your monkey, squirrel, cat – Your dog or bird – no matter what; Only your favourite let me be'.[108] They also centre the poet's literary gifts, but with the addition of a striking material dimension. When writing to women, Charles often sends his verses as an accompaniment to a gift – usually a book or poem, though he also occasionally sends edibles – which is referenced in the poem's title. In the verses, he reflects on the transformative effect that consuming the gift might have on the recipient's moral and emotional development, and offers guidance as to the form it should take. Such a stance significantly complicates the dynamic of solicitation.

Take, for example, the 'Ode, sent to the Miss Gordons, with The Goodnatur'd Man, A Comedy, by Dr Goldsmith'. Charles uses these verses to raise the topic of critical taste:

> If Goldsmith's humour, wit and ease
> Your nicer tastes and judgment please,
> No longer shall the Bard complain
> Of critics impotent and vain:
> But should it be the Poet's fate
> To raise disgust, or fire your hate;
> Or should the piece your Fancies cloy
> Then use it – as the Greeks did Troy.[109]

While this poem is ostensibly deferential to the young ladies' critical opinions, Charles also uses it to draw attention to his own literary gifts. His mention

---

[106] 'Verses sent in a Letter to Ensign Simon Macdonald', Osborn c37, 49–50.
[107] 'Written in the Works of Anacreon', Osborn c35, 39–40. See Stockdale's letters to Charles of 31 January 1780 and 20 November 1780, Osborn c6.
[108] 'Verses sent to the Miss Willox's, with some Fruit', Osborn c38, 37–39.
[109] 'Ode, sent to the Miss Gordons', Osborn c38, 30.

of himself, the 'Poet', is linked metrically with Goldsmith's 'Bard', thereby establishing a connection with the famous playwright which is also reflected in the double gift of the published play and the manuscript poem. The verses also imply that both 'Bard' and 'Poet' have had experience of 'Critics impotent and vain' – the poet's frustration is exercised not only on Goldsmith's behalf but also, it seems, on his own.

Then there is 'Sonnet Addressed to Miss Rachel and Miss Jessy Willox, Prefaced to the Epistles from Euphrasia to Castalio; and from Edwin to Angelina'.[110] In this poem, Charles declares his certainty that if they peruse his own poetic portrayals of 'A Lovers' sorrows, and a Lady's sighs', Rachel and Jessy's 'gentle hearts' cannot remain 'unmoved'. 'Then fear not', he instructs them, 'if a rising sigh displays / Your worth of mind, and tenderness of heart'. The reader then experiences an abrupt transition to the poet's contemplation of his own prospective literary fame:

> Should Fame my brow with laurel wreaths entwine
> Should praise immortal wait upon my songs,
> To you, with joy, my honours I resign –
> Yours is the lay – to you the praise belongs.

Again, in 'Ode sent with the Memoirs of Miss Sidney Biddulph to the Miss Willoxes', there is similar certainty that Frances Sheridan's narrative cannot fail to 'impart' the protagonist's sufferings to 'the generous heart'. But even as this poem is initially framed as addressing Rachel and Jessy's responses to the text, it is really Charles's own literary sensibility that he wants to display. 'For heavenly transports bless *his* mind, Who lives – the friend of human kind: Whose soul Compassion's law has taught, And with the noblest feelings fraught'[111] [italics mine].

In a sensitive study of Elizabeth Montagu's reading networks, Markman Ellis contends that disseminating books as gifts is 'an important signal in the economy of patronage and sycophancy'.[112] These brief examples demonstrate how Charles sent decidedly mixed signals, uneasily blending the position of bardic sycophancy with a tone of authoritative critical instruction. Having established Charles's general circulatory practice in this respect, in the next section I turn to the specific printed text that he embellished with manuscript poetry most frequently – and strikingly – to burnish his social standing. This, of course, is *Evelina*. Such practice emerged from a specific set of

---

[110] Osborn c38, 17–18. The 'Epistle from Euphrasia to Castalio', and 'The Shepherd's Return' were Charles's own poems. See Osborn c38, 19–25 and 7–8.

[111] 'Ode sent with the Memoirs of Miss Sidney Biddulph', Osborn c38, 40–41.

[112] Ellis, 'Reading Practices', 217.

circumstances in which alienation, insecurity, and ambition all met in Charles Burney's poetic output. To understand why this was, we need to turn to his sister's novel.

2 Charles and *Evelina*

Evelina was published in January 1778, and Frances Burney's identity as the author was revealed in June. Her subsequent celebrity has been extensively documented.[113] It is worth noting that the teenage Charles could claim a minuscule share of the credit for bringing *Evelina* to publication, since in 1776–77, he had helped Frances to preserve her anonymity with Lowndes by acting as a disguised go-between under the assumed name of 'Mr King'.[114] While many scholars have noted this fact, they have not contextualised Charles's early performance as part of a broader picture of ambivalent promotional practice. Charles would continue, following *Evelina*'s publication, to facilitate its circulation and bolster its reputation. Simultaneously, he would attempt to superimpose his own performed identity over that of his author-sister.

This section of the Element reconstructs Charles's engagements with three different sets of *Evelina* between 1777 and 1781. For convenience, I call these texts the Shinfield *Evelina*, the Aberdeen *Evelina*, and the Banff *Evelina*, and structure my narrative accordingly. I then turn to examine a 1779 third edition of the novel held in Special Collections at the University of Aberdeen (hereafter called the SC set), arguing that idiosyncratic marginalia identify it as the very copy that Charles lent around Banff. This provides necessary context for Sections 3–6, in which Charles is more closely considered as prefixer, reader, and loaner.

2.1 The Shinfield *Evelina*

Charles read *Evelina* for the first time during the spring of 1778.[115] His correspondence with Frances indicates that he tried to borrow a set from a circulating library in Reading, but ultimately ended up reading one that she sent to him from London.[116] As briefly noted in Section 1, two different fragments from Charles to Frances dating from this period survive, both of which mention his early response to *Evelina*. In the first, he notes at the head of the page, 'I have read Evelina, & like it *vastely* [sic] much', before proceeding to correct her translation of Seneca. At the foot, he adds a postscript: 'This [the

---

[113] Hemlow, *History,* 91–104.   [114] Hemlow, *History,* 64, 100. See also *EJL* 2:214, n. 39.

[115] Frances mentions that Charles 'never saw it in MSS' in Frances Burney to Charles Burney, [8 July 1778], *EJL* 3:51.

[116] See the end of the second fragment for my evidence.

letter] shall accompany Evelina, which *the Parson* is reading.'[117] The second fragment is more detailed:

> I think the Letter which describes the Meeting of Evelina, & Sir John Belmont is the best written in the Book; & the horror & remorse, which must almost necessarily attend such a meeting, is very admirably described. Mrs Francis cried when she read it – She admires it much I can promise you – & launched out in the praise of the unknown Writer. I, as you know, am not at all *smoaky* – So it went off very well: She c[d] not eat any dinner, while she was engaged in reading it – In the Ode, I believe that glows would after, of, have been more elegant, had it been glow, but the Verse, or rather Rhime, w[d] not allow it.
>
> I like Evelina excessively: I am not fond of Novels in general; &, those of Richardson, Fielding, & Smollett being excepted, there is scarcely one I w[d] ever wish to read again – to those Authors' works, I must now add Miss B–'s productions – Pray whose set is this, which you have sent me? It is not the one you mentioned: pray answer me this question – I hope you will not be offended at my criticisms, I did not look for faults . . .[118]

In Section 1, I noted that the form of the Seneca letter works to subordinate Frances's creative achievement to Charles's critical expertise. This second fragment, I think, effectively does the same thing. While his overall tone is complimentary, Charles also offers 'criticisms' of the 'faults' he detects, particularly in the prefatory Ode. His airy aside that he is 'not fond of novels in general' also serves as a backhanded compliment, reminding Frances of the lowbrow form she has chosen even as he condescends to place her with its acknowledged masters.

It is easy to imagine that Charles may have had mixed feelings about his sister's literary success, and that he might have found it galling to compare their situations. Drawing on Hester Thrale's sharp observation about the Burney siblings – 'their Esteem & fondness for the Dr. seems to inspire them all with a Desire not to disgrace him; & so every individual of [the family] must write and read & be literary' – Margaret Doody has argued convincingly that throughout their lives the Burney children remained desperate to please their father through literary achievements and honours.[119] Other biographers have speculated that Dr Burney's enthusiasm for promoting Frances's celebrity at this time stemmed partly from embarrassment at the spectacular fall from grace of his budding scholar.[120] Charles's own career prospects looked extremely uncertain during 1778, when, as he wrote to his school friend Francis Wollaston, he was 'Forced to relinquish every fondest hope / My time in vile obscurity to

---

[117] Charles Burney to Frances Burney, undated, OSB MSS 3, Box 6, Folder 379.

[118] Undated and unattributed fragment labelled 'Note on Evelina in unknown hand, post 1777', OSB MSS 3 Box 5 f. 346.

[119] Doody, *The Life in the Works,* 21.   [120] Hemlow, *History,* 244.

waste'.[121] The brevity of his recognition of Frances's achievement, and the high-handed tone he takes to 'correct' her prose, might therefore credibly be attributed to envy, stemming from a feeling of comparative inferiority. If so, it indicates an early propensity in Charles to see his sister's literary success as related, or at least relatable, to his own intellectual prowess, and to deploy a gendered belletristic persona in an attempt to reassert himself.

Tellingly, Charles also declares in this fragment, after describing Mrs Francis 'launching out in the praise of the unknown Writer', that he is 'not at all *smoaky* – so it went off very well'. At this time, the slang word 'smoaky' could signify bad temper, shrewdness, suspicion, ridicule, or jealousy.[122] Charles probably means that he did not act suspiciously when lending the book to Mrs Francis, thus preserving the secret of Frances's authorship. But the multiple valences of the word, coupled with his assiduous corrections, suggest that he may have felt envy or chagrin alongside other, more positive fraternal emotions.

I want to draw three more observations out of these fragments as evidence of Charles's readerly practice. First, his usage of the term '*vastely* much' indicates a casual yet striking mimicry. Where words are underlined and deliberately misspelled in Burney family correspondence, there is always the possibility that the misspelling is an in-joke, part of the elaborate family dialect (a mixture of slang, pet names, mimicry, and code) that makes their letters such a challenge to edit.[123] On this occasion, 'vastely' is an echo of the distinctive lexicon of the indefatigable Madame Duval, a character in *Evelina* who makes liberal use of that term: possibly with the spelling altered to imply a strong French accent.[124] Duval was one of the characters most loved and imitated by the novel's early readers, and Charles's letter hints that, like other readers, he couldn't resist the temptation to 'perform' his sister's memorable antagonist.

Second, we find a hint of identification (rather than performance) in Charles's remark that 'the horror & remorse, which must almost necessarily attend such a meeting is very admirably described'. In singling out the confrontation scene between Sir John Belmont and Evelina, Charles largely focuses on Mrs Francis's sentimental response, but also adds his own assessment of its *veracity*.

---

[121] 'A Verse Letter to F.J.H.W.', OSB MSS 3, Box 7, Folder 480.

[122] *Oxford English Dictionary*, s.v. 'smoky, adj., sense 10', July 2023. https://doi.org/10.1093/OED/1499609200.

[123] Examples of this tendency abound throughout the Burney family correspondence. See Erickson, 'Esther Sleepe', 27.

[124] See, for example, Madame Duval's contention that Parisian gentlemen are 'vastly too polite' to notice a woman's age (Burney, *Evelina,* 61); her protestation that she would have 'liked [the opera] vastly' if she had been in the pit (95) or her mocking Sir Clement for being 'vastly polite all of a sudden' (211).

Usage of the emphatic 'must', immediately qualified by the self-conscious 'almost necessarily', hints at first-hand knowledge of such strong emotions, raising the possibility that he may have been thinking of a confrontation with his own father following his disgrace. Although reversing the generational positions, Charles appears to be reading his life, affectively speaking, into Frances's work.

Other striking aspects of Charles's treatment of the Shinfield *Evelina* are his interest in who else is reading the book and his commitment to extending its readership. In the first fragment, Charles refers to '*the Parson*' (perhaps the Rev. Mr. Jane, who Charles satirised in his poetry as 'the little Welsh curate') reading *Evelina*, while in the second, he describes Mrs Francis's response. This indicates that Charles was alert to the novel's readership within Shinfield and suggests that he was actively subletting his own borrowed copy before returning it to his sister ('This shall accompany Evelina'). This would be consonant with his later documented practice in Scotland.

Finally – though Charles does not mention it in these fragments – we should note that his first reading of *Evelina* acted as a stimulant to poetic composition. As I show in Section 3, the all-important sonnet that he reports 'prefixing' to *Evelina* and lending around Aberdeen was first composed in Shinfield. Its first title was not 'The Female Reader' but 'Sonnet Written in a Blank Leaf of Evelina', and its likely first recipient was Frances Burney herself.

2.2 The Aberdeen *Evelina*

In the spring of 1779, Charles announced to Frances that 'Evelina is in Aberdeen'.[125] Having returned the Shinfield *Evelina* to its author, once settled in Aberdeen, he again turned to 'a Circulating Library' to obtain his own set – this time successfully. Charles does not name the library, but there were two in operation in Aberdeen at this time: John Boyle's and Alexander Angus's.[126] While to my knowledge no catalogue survives for Boyle's, there are several for Angus's, the 'showiest shop in town' and 'favourite rendezvous of many of the respectable citizens of Aberdeen', which was based at the Narrow Wynd.[127] One catalogue is dated 1779 and features an entry for *Evelina: Or, the History of a Young Lady's Entrance into the World*, priced at nine shillings.[128]

Charles's account of his lending practice is quoted in my Introduction and will be interrogated in Section 5, but we are now in a better position to extract a few key features. In Aberdeen, he establishes a lending network on a broader

---

[125] Charles Burney to Frances Burney, undated, OSB MSS 3, Box 6, Folder 381.

[126] Alston, *Libraries in Scotland*. See also Fox, *The Press and the People*, Chapter 4.

[127] Lawrance, *An Old Book-Selling Firm*, 10–11.

[128] University of Aberdeen, (SC) SBL 1779 NP 2, 21.

scale than his Shinfield circle, and when gathering responses, he is particularly interested in which characters draw readers' admiration. Advertising his sister's authorship is a key component of his promotional practice: 'They are all in raptures with it – & all longing to see *you* … [Gordon] says, he is sure that Miss Burney's pen would have made a great deal of it.'[129] Consonant with the fact that Frances Burney's authorship was now common knowledge, this differs from his practice in Shinfield, where he kept the authorship a secret from Mrs Francis. Finally, one of his compliments – 'Every body is surprised at the Performance' – is, like his comment about not being fond of novels, decidedly backhanded, especially when followed by a boast about his own 'prefixed' poem, which 'likewise had its *admirers*'. These concluding lines recall the interplay of various dynamics in Charles's response to the Shinfield *Evelina*, and hint at a feature of his circulatory practice addressed in the next section: his desire to not only share space with his sister on the page but also superimpose his literary identity alongside or over hers.

The Willoxes, Gordons, and Gerards are not the only members of Charles's Aberdeen circle to whom he promotes the novel and its author. Letters from his tutor James Dunbar and friend Percival Stockdale also indicate that they had read or discussed the novel with Charles. Both men write from London, where he has encouraged them to pay a visit to his family, and both refer to the flesh-and-blood Frances Burney herself, when they encounter her, as 'Evelina'.[130] This conflation of the author with the heroine indicates that Charles not only promoted his sister's novel but also encouraged prospective readers to identify her with her protagonist.

2.3 The Banff *Evelina*

When Charles went on a walking tour around North East Scotland in the summer of 1780, he took a set of *Evelina* with him. Staying at the home of his friend James Likly, he notes, 'read[ing] Evelina to the Misses [Likly's sisters], neither of whom have charms to promote flirtation'.[131] He left his set in Banff, in the custody of the more desirable Mary Rose, when he returned to Aberdeen in the autumn of 1780, and did not recover it until spring 1781 (if at all).[132] The novel was clearly on his mind as he travelled, since he uses it to characterise the people he meets along the way. A Mrs Admiral Gordon is 'a

---

129 Charles Burney to Frances Burney, undated, OSB MSS 3, Box 6, Folder 381.

130 James Dunbar to Charles Burney, 24 May 1779, OSB MSS 3, Box 9, Folder 670; Percival Stockdale to Charles Burney, 25 September 1779 and 31 January 1780, Osborn c6.

131 Charles Burney, Journal-letter to his sister, Susan Elizabeth (Burney) Phillips, 1780, OSB MSS 3 Box 7, Folder 442, 10; Walker, 'Charles Burney's Tour', 3.

132 'Mrs Rose sends her compts & Evelina, who has visited much this Winter in Banff will come & pay her dutyfull respects to you soon.' Charles Cordiner to Charles Burney, 24 February 1781, OSB MSS 3, Box 9, Folder 633.

little in the Mrs Beaumont style, all for the nobility'; this is a reference to the 'Court Calendar bigot' Mrs Beaumont in *Evelina*.[133]

It is unlikely that the set Charles took to Banff in the summer of 1780 was the same one circulated in Aberdeen in the spring of 1779.[134] Instead, I think it likely that it was a third copy, which Charles again obtained directly from Frances Burney in London. My evidence for this is contained in two separate letters. As already mentioned, when Charles's tutor James Dunbar travelled to London in the spring of 1779, Charles arranged for him to pay the Burney family a visit. 'You have long ere this, I take it for granted, seen Mr Dunbar,' he writes to Frances. '. . . Pray will you give into his care the set of Evelina'.[135] Furthermore, in a letter of 24 May 1779, Dunbar reports back to Charles, 'I am just come from dining at Dr. Burney's, where I have met w[h] the utmost Civility – I shall remember your commission about Evelina, more interesting surely from having seen the Original'.[136] The implication is clear: in 1779 Charles had asked Dunbar to bring him a set of *Evelina* that was currently in the possession of his family, and so it was probably this family set that he took to Banff in 1780.

2.4 The SC Set: Markings and 'Moor Fowls'

In the University of Aberdeen's Special Collections, there is a battered three-volume set of the 1779 third edition of *Evelina*.[137] Its early provenance, bibliographically speaking, is a mystery. Supralibros, pressmarks, and bookplates indicate only the ownership of King's College and of the University of Aberdeen (formed after King's and Marischal combined in 1860).[138] The Library's manuscript catalogues provide only the barest information, indicating that the set entered the King's collection before 1848.[139] In short, there is no concrete bibliographical evidence that this is *not* one of Charles Burney's *Evelina*s: but there is also no evidence that it *is*. However, idiosyncratic marginal annotation within the first and third volumes suggest strongly that this is the very set which Charles took with him to Banff.

---

[133] Charles Burney, Journal-letter to his sister, Susan Elizabeth (Burney) Phillips, 1780, OSB MSS 3 Box 7, Folder 442, 47. Walker, 'Charles Burney's Tour', 13; Burney, *Evelina*, 284.

[134] The maximum term for which one could borrow a book from Angus's was one year, which Charles would have exceeded by the time he set out for Banff in 1780. In addition, the title recorded in Angus's Catalogue suggests a second edition while, as I argue in subsequent sections, the copy taken to Banff was a third edition.

[135] Charles Burney to Frances Burney, undated, Box 6, Folder 381, OSB MSS 3.

[136] James Dunbar to Charles Burney, 24 May 1779, OSB MSS 3, Box 9, Folder 670.

[137] University of Aberdeen, SB 82366 E1.

[138] Email from Michelle Gait to Sophie Coulombeau, 23 November 2020.

[139] University of Aberdeen, KINGS 5/1/1/14 p.438. There is no record of its donation as a gift or bequest.

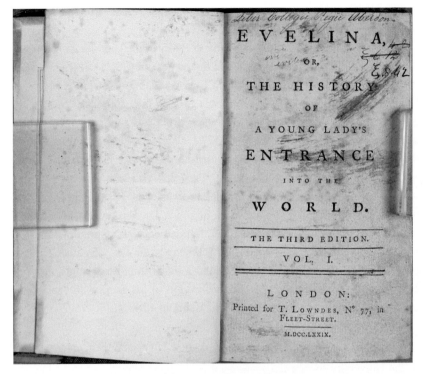

Figure 2 Title page and preceding verso.
Frances Burney, *Evelina, or, the History of a Young Lady's Entrance into the World*
(London: Lowndes, third edition, 1779), vol. 1, unpaginated. Aberdeen, University of
Aberdeen, SB 82366 E1.

2.4.1 Markings

The most notable thing about the volumes is how roughly they have been treated.
On the title page of the first volume, we find heavy ink smudges in two separate
places, while on the facing verso there is light pitted residue, roughly positioned
in a mirror image to the heaviest smudging (see Figure 2). More smudges and
blots, both brown and black, occur frequently throughout the three volumes.
There are numerous grease stains, probably often deposits left by human fingers.
Pages are occasionally rumpled or folded over, while one leaf (pages 71–72 in the
first volume) is badly mutilated, with three-quarters of the page ripped away on
a diagonal. On page 46 of the second volume, there is an abrasion in the paper, the
edges of which appear to be singed; perhaps a burn from a hastily extinguished
cinder. A hole in the page occurs on page 85 of the second volume.

Not all markings are accidental. Doodles and underlines abound. There are also
several annotations, made in both black ink and faded pencil. On page 94 of the first
volume, alongside a debate between Madame Duval and Captain Mirvan about age

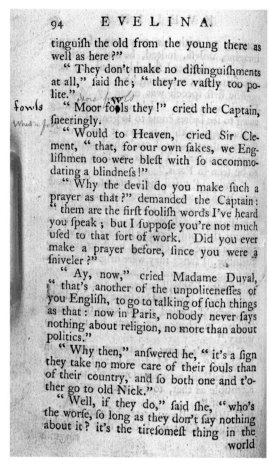

Figure 3 Marginalia concerning moor fowl.
Frances Burney, *Evelina, or, the History of a Young Lady's Entrance into the World*
(London: Lowndes, third edition, 1779), vol. 1, p. 94. Aberdeen, University of Aberdeen,
SB 82366 E1.

and beauty, a brief marginal dialogue seems to have taken place between two readers (see Figure 3). The text under annotation is the Captain's exclamation, rendered in this edition as 'Moor fools they!' 'Moor' is a printer's error; in subsequent editions, the phrase would read, '*More* fools they!' [Italics mine].

It would not be unusual to find a reader hand-correcting such a typo; a tendency elegantly described by the Multigraph Collective as 'testimony to an editorial mind-set fostered by print culture'.[140] Indeed, there are incidences of such corrections in this very set – for example, in the third volume, someone has corrected the antiquated usage 'you was' to the more modern 'you were'.

---

[140] Multigraph Collective, *Interacting with Print*, 211.

However, in the case of 1:94, a marginal annotator, writing in black ink, has responded chaotically rather than correctively. Instead of correcting the mis-spelling 'moor' to 'more', they have deliberately amended 'fools' to read 'fowls'. The word 'fowls' is then written a second time in the margin, perhaps to avoid any misunderstanding. 'More fools' has become 'Moor fowls', in an intriguing instance of what the Multigraph Collective terms 'disruption', whereby a satirical reader 'turn[s] the fallible, error-prone nature of printing to their advantage'.[141] A faint pencil hand, presumably later, has tried to correct the disruption, replacing 'Moor fowls' with 'More fools' and writing in the margin, 'What a fool'. It is unclear whether this remark refers to the Captain, the subject of his utterance, or the disruptive annotator.

A black ink hand and a pencil hand – possibly, though not certainly, the same ones – meet once again on the final page of volume 3. If indeed the same annotators as those on 1:94, they are in closer accord with their satisfied responses to *Evelina*'s happy ending (see Figure 4). Beneath the printed 'FINIS', the pencil hand provides an approving verdict: 'The most delightful novel I ever read.' Meanwhile, the black ink hand attempts to provide the last word on the question of Evelina's ambiguous surname (possibilities raised throughout the narrative include Anville, Villars, and Belmont). When the protagonist signs her final letter to Mr Villars 'EVELINA', the annotator takes advantage of the space afforded by the margin to add, 'ORVILLE'. A decorative underlining flourish unites the print given name with the manuscript surname. The annotator, clearly just as alert as modern critics to the significance of naming within the plot, thereby uses the annotation to elevate Evelina's conjugal identity as wife to Lord Orville above the other roles she has played throughout the narrative (daughter to Mr Villars or Sir John Belmont, brother to Macartney, granddaughter to Madame Duval, etc.). In doing so, they stake a claim to 'insider knowledge ... that qualifie[s] them as collaborators in the finalization of the book'.[142]

There is one more annotation of significance. In my bibliographical assessment of the SC *Evelina*, I suggested that the set contains no ownership inscription – but there is one possible, peculiar exception. At the end of the third volume, on an advertise-ment for a miscellany called the 'Theatrical Bouquet' also published by Lowndes, a black ink hand has written at the top of the page, 'Evelina Anville' (See Figure 5).

The nature of this annotation is far from clear. However, given its positioning on the paratextual fringe of the volume – alongside an advertisement specifically raising the topic of theatrical performance – it is possibly intended as a joke ownership inscription. Katharina Rennhak has noted how paratexts can 'swing

---

[141] Multigraph Collective, *Interacting with Print*, 98–99.
[142] Multigraph Collective, *Interacting with Print*, 205.

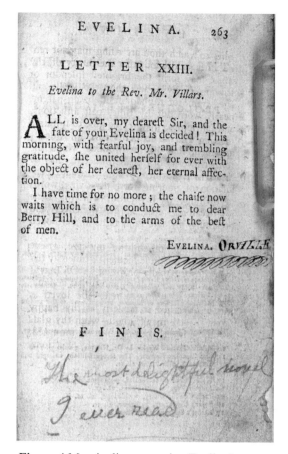

Figure 4 Marginalia concerning Evelina's name.
Frances Burney, *Evelina, or, the History of a Young Lady's Entrance into the World*
(London: Lowndes, third edition, 1779), vol. 3, p. 263. Aberdeen, University of
Aberdeen, SB 82366 E1.

wide open the door on the threshold between the extratextual and the textual …
between authentic prefatorial figures on the one hand and fictive characters on the
other'.[143] In a similar metatextual act of play, the black ink annotator may be
indicating that this set of the novel belongs, in some way, to the fictional heroine.[144]

Tempting though it may be, I cannot conclusively attribute the black ink hand of
'moor fowl', 'Orville', or 'Evelina Anville' to Charles Burney on purely palaeographic grounds. Although both the letters on 1:94 and those on 3:263 bear some

---

[143] Rennhak, 'Paratexts and the Construction of Author Identities', 63.

[144] The Multigraph Collective notes that in the Romantic period it would be more common for an
ownership inscription to be positioned at the front of a book than the back (*Interacting with
Print*, 210–11). But, as David Pearson shows, this is far from a universal practice. (Pearson,
Provenance Research, 20–21).

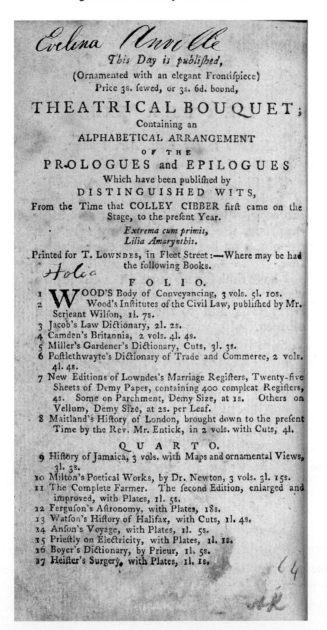

Evelina Anville

This Day is published,

(Ornamented with an elegant Frontifpiece)
Price 3s. fewed, or 3s. 6d. bound,

THEATRICAL BOUQUET;

Containing an

ALPHABETICAL ARRANGEMENT

OF THE

PROLOGUES and EPILOGUES

Which have been publifhed by

DISTINGUISHED WITS,

From the Time that COLLEY CIBBER firft came on the
Stage, to the prefent Year.

Extrema cum primis,
Lilia Amarynthis.

Printed for T. LOWNDES, in Fleet Street:—Where may be had
the following Books.

Holic

FOLIO.

1 WOOD'S Body of Conveyancing, 3 vols. 5l. 10s.
2   Wood's Inftitutes of the Civil Law, publifhed by Mr.
   Serjeant Wilfon, 1l. 7s.
3 Jacob's Law Dictionary, 2l. 2s.
4 Camden's Britannia, 2 vols. 4l. 4s.
5 Miller's Gardener's Dictionary, Cuts, 3l. 3s.
6 Poftlethwayte's Dictionary of Trade and Commerce, 2 vols.
   4l. 4s.
7 New Editions of Lowndes's Marriage Regifters, Twenty-five
   Sheets of Demy Paper, containing 400 compleat Regifters,
   4s.   Some on Parchment, Demy Size, at 1s.   Others on
   Vellum, Demy Size, at 2s. per Leaf.
8 Maitland's Hiftory of London, brought down to the prefent
   Time by the Rev. Mr. Entick, in 2 vols. with Cuts, 4l.

QUARTO.

9 Hiftory of Jamaica, 3 vols. with Maps and ornamental Views,
   3l. 3s.
10 Milton's Poetical Works, by Dr. Newton, 3 vols. 3l. 15s.
11 The Complete Farmer. The fecond Edition, enlarged and
   improved, with Plates, 1l. 5s.
12 Ferguson's Aftronomy, with Plates, 18s.
13 Watfon's Hiftory of Halifax, with Cuts, 1l. 4s.
14 Anfon's Voyage, with Plates, 1l. 5s.
15 Prieftly on Electricity, with Plates, 1l. 1s.
16 Boyer's Dictionary, by Prieur, 1l. 5s.
17 Heifter's Surgery, with Plates, 1l. 1s.

Figure 5 Annotation, 'Evelina Anville'.

Frances Burney, *Evelina, or, the History of a Young Lady's Entrance into the World*
(London: Lowndes, third edition, 1779), vol. 3, advertisement, unpaginated. Aberdeen,
University of Aberdeen, SB 82366 E1.

resemblance to his cuneive hand in other documents, they also include certain deliberately stylised features which I have not encountered, such as the backward serifs and crossbars on the capital letters. These examples are too brief and too stylised to provide points of meaningful comparison with his hand in letters and poems of the same period. The annotation 'Evelina Anville', however, provides a much stronger likeness to Charles's proven hand during the early 1780s. If we compare the word 'Evelina' in the SC set annotation (Figure 5) to Charles's 'Evelina' in his miscellany (Figure 7), we can see that, while the annotator has a better pen and is taking more care to write neatly, the letters are formed in identical proportions and in almost precisely the same ways. Personally, therefore, I think it likely that Charles provided at least one of the black ink annotations, but on strictly palaeographic grounds I cannot be certain.

Happily, the annotations' content provides a more compelling case for Charles's identity as an annotator, which can only complement the tantalising palaeographic similarities. His desire to impose a reading of the text as a sentimental romance (see Sections 3–5) fits neatly with the annotator's desire on 3:263 to stress Evelina's conjugal identity in her final signoff. The fact that he had previously encouraged his friends to identify 'Frances Burney' with 'Evelina Anville' (see Section 2) reflects the logic of inscribing Frances's book with Evelina's name on the advertisement. But by far the strongest evidence of his involvement concerns the idiosyncratic nature of the 'moor fowl' annotation on 1:94, which, when read alongside Charles's archive from the late summer of 1780, indicates that he or one of his Banff friends is the black ink hand, and that the SC copy and the Banff *Evelina* are one and the same. To explain the significance of this remark, it is necessary to turn to the moment in the plot of *Evelina* where the first annotator decides to intervene.

2.4.2 Moor fowl

On a visit to Ranelagh, Madame Duval and the Captain debate the motivations behind the trend for ladies wearing large hats. The Captain opines 'that they were invented by some wrinkled old hag, who'd a mind for to keep the young fellows in chace.' Madame Duval retorts that 'in Paris no woman need n't be at such a trouble as that, to be taken very genteel notice of'.

> 'Why, will you pretend for to say', returned the Captain, 'that they don't distinguish the old from the young there as well as here?'
> 'They don't make no distinguishments at all', said she; 'they're vastly too polite'.
> 'More fools they!' said the Captain, sneeringly.[145]

---

[145] Burney, *Evelina*, 61.

Once the annotation is implemented, we are left with the cryptic formulation 'Moor fowls they!' and the baffling proposition that French gentlemen, over-chivalrous to a ludicrous degree, resemble, or are interchangeable with, moor fowl. This is not particularly edifying, until we familiarise ourselves with Charles Burney's correspondence of the late summer of 1780, and it becomes apparent that chivalry and moor fowl were both much on his mind.

During this time, Charles was the guest of Fife – a keen huntsman – at his country retreat, Mar Lodge. Charles had also recently made the acquaintance of Fife's factor, William Rose, and Rose's wife, Mary. Mary Rose was renowned as an extraordinary beauty, and Charles – possibly on the rebound from Jessy Willox's shock engagement – was smitten. He writes to his sisters, 'she baffles all description, nor does the Painter exist who could do justice to such perfection.'[146] He also gave vent to his feelings in two poems written during July: 'The Rose' and 'The Secret Lover, A Song'. 'The Rose' is dedicated to Mary, and, while respectfully courtly, was probably written for circulation. I doubt the same is true of 'The Secret Lover', in which Charles laments that he must 'conceal the soft alarms / Nor breathe my fond desire'. In August, he writes Mary a third poem: 'Epistle to a Lady, with a present of Moor Fowl'.

What does moor fowl have to do with this? The answer lies in a series of letters written between Charles, Fife, and the Roses over August and September. In letters to his factor, Fife made a running joke of the fact that he could not prevail upon Charles to go hunting with him, since he obstinately preferred to stay at Mar Lodge 'ever at Books, and pen and ink'.[147] Meanwhile, writing to William Rose, Charles readily admits his inability or reluctance to kill game, ruefully describing himself as 'not a very bloodthirsty shot'.[148] Despite such queasiness, Fife would generally give Charles the honour of naming the local lady to whom the spoils should be sent for cooking: one letter relates his 'direct' choice 'without a moment's hesitation' for Mrs Rose to receive some venison.[149] When, at the end of August, Fife eventually managed to drag his guest out shooting, Charles records how he was a 'tame spectator' at the death of some moor fowl. It seems that on this occasion the custom was observed and the usual recipient named. The present of moor fowl was accompanied by Charles's poem, which survives in two

---

[146] Charles Burney, Journal-letter to his sister, Susan Elizabeth (Burney) Phillips, 1780, OSB MSS 3 Box 7, Folder 442, 37; Walker, 'Charles Burney's Tour', 11. 'The Rose', Osborn c35, 55–6; 'The Secret Lover', Osborn c35, 59–60.

[147] Fife to William Rose, 13 August 1780 and 25 August 1780. See Tayler and Tayler, *Lord Fife and his Factor*, 124–130.

[148] Charles Burney to William Rose, 25 August 1780, University of Aberdeen, MS 2226.

[149] Tayler and Tayler, *Lord Fife and his Factor*, 125.

versions: one in the original letter to Mary Rose, and the other in a revised and polished version in one of Charles's notebooks.[150]

In both versions, the poem recounts the mock-heroic hunt of Charles and his host, who pass over mountains 'with steps as nimble / As if in size, 'twas but a thimble' in pursuit of their prey. When they finally shoot (or Fife does, at least), 'whole *Covies* met their fate', and the huntsman 'heard / Or seem'd to hear – the dying Bird / Who thus in feeble accents tried / To move our pity, ere He died'. The moor fowl's dying wish is to be eaten by the fairest of the fair: Mary Rose.

> Say, Man, to you what pleasure flows,
> Thus to molest our calm repose,
> And with blood-thirsty souls profane
> The limits of our ancient reign? –
> But hear me, ere I yield my breath –
> Hear the request I make in death:
> Since, cruel Wretches, ye would slay me,
> To Mrs Rose – Duff House – convey me.
> If she'll accept us – send her all,
> Who victims to your fury fall.
> To think that she the gift receives,
> A balm to ease our torture gives;
> And should she find us dainty food,
> You not in vain have shed our blood:
> For happily our lives we close,
> To gain a smile from Mrs Rose!

The poem concludes by drawing a bathetic comparison between the hyperbolically chivalrous fowl, relishing his own imminent consumption, and the poet himself, who initially rushes to lay down his own life alongside the bird's but then backtracks, sheepishly confessing, 'if blest with ease, / Life would a *little longer* please'. Though self-awareness is not usually Charles's strong point in his poetry, this one suggests that, on occasion, he could laugh at the models of masculinity that shaped his poetic, sociable, and recreational practice. His wry letter to William Rose, dated a week or two after the game and the poem were sent, indicates that the moor fowl did not cope well with the excessive summer heat: 'I am very sorry that the Moor Fowl were obliged to be returned to the place from which they came – and that the mountains should receive, what was intended for the dinner of Mrs Rose. How vain are human expectations!'[151]

---

[150] 'Epistle to a Lady, with a present of Moor Fowl', Osborn c35, 62–65, and 'Letter (in verse)', University of Aberdeen, MS 997/2/17. All quotations are taken from the Aberdeen version.
[151] Charles Burney to William Rose, 5 September 1780, University of Aberdeen, MS 2226.

This same letter indicates that Mary Rose had declared an intention to send Charles some verses of her own in response to his compliment.[152] Sadly, these have not survived. However, we do know that she borrowed the Banff *Evelina* from Charles over the winter of 1780, that the two of them had a running joke about moor fowl, and that there is a handwritten annotation in the SC set, which, within the context of Charles's poem and correspondence, makes a sort of sense. Though the precise resonances are impossible to recover, this marginalia raises tantalising possibilities: that Mary Rose saw the funny side of the gift and poem; that she and Charles conducted their mock-courtly flirtation in print as well as manuscript spaces; and that the Banff set of the novel, arriving back at King's College after Charles's departure, was absorbed into the Library's collection.[153] If so, then the copy of *Evelina* still held today by the University of Aberdeen was once in the custody of not only Charles but also Frances Burney. Or, if we adopt the logic of James Dunbar and Percival Stockdale, and also of the volume's possible ownership inscription, of 'Evelina Anville'.

3 Prefixing *Evelina*

I have been unable to locate any surviving version of Charles's sonnet which bears either the title 'To the Female Reader' or physical evidence of having once been 'prefixed' to a set of *Evelina*. However, two copies survive, both carefully dated. One is in the hand of Charlotte Anne Broome, Charles and Frances's youngest sister, in a family verse miscellany in the Houghton Library (hereafter referred to as the Harvard version, see Figure 6). There it is entitled 'Sonnet Written in a Blank Leaf of Evelina', attributed to 'Charles Burney, D.D', and dated October 1778.[154] I copy this version below. The other is written into Charles's miscellany 'Poetical Trifles' in the Beinecke Library (hereafter referred to as the Yale version, see Figure 7). There it is entitled 'Sonnet, written in Evelina, and Addressed to the Ladies', and dated April 1779.[155]

---

[152] 'I am very happy at the thought of my Muse inviting Mrs Rose's to come forth from her secret residence. I shall wait impatiently for the arrival of the Messenger next week, in hopes of being favoured with a sight of the production.' Charles Burney to William Rose, 5 September 1780, University of Aberdeen, MS 2226.

[153] Such a novel would not have been considered an inappropriate holding for a university library. As the *Books and Borrowing* database shows, *Evelina* was borrowed from several Scottish university libraries throughout the 1770s and 1780s. See *Books and Borrowing: An Analysis of Scottish Borrowers' Registers, 1750–1830*, s.v., 'Simple search for "Date of borrowing: 1770–1790, Book title: Evelina",' accessed 27 February 2024, https://borrowing.stir.ac.uk/search/p-1/0/0/simple/bdate|1770_1790/bookname|Evelina.

[154] Charlotte Francis, *Commonplace book*, MS Eng 926, 106–107. See Clark, 'Growing Up Burney'.

[155] Osborn c35, 29–30. This version is also reproduced as Appendix 2 in *EJL* 3.

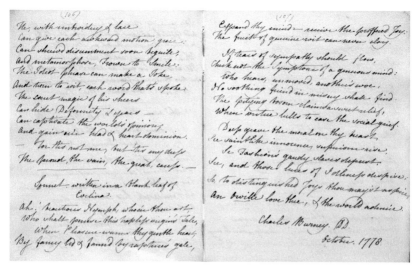

Figure 6 Harvard version of Charles's sonnet, October 1778.
Charles Burney, 'Sonnet, written in a blank leaf of *Evelina*', October 1778, in Charlotte A. Francis, (Charlotte Anne), *Commonplace book of poetry: manuscript* [1771–1806 and undated], pp. 106–7. Cambridge, Mass., Harvard University, Houghton Library, MS Eng 926.

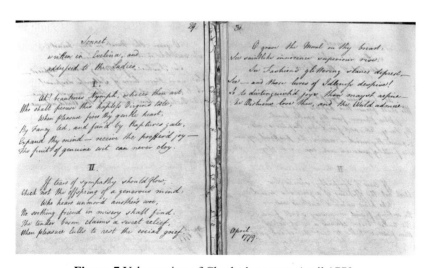

Figure 7 Yale version of Charles's sonnet, April 1779.
Charles Burney, 'Sonnet, written in Evelina and addressed to the Ladies', Charles Burney, *Poetical trifles* [1781], pp. 29–30. New Haven, Yale University, Beinecke Rare Book and Manuscript Library, The James Marshall and Marie-Louise Osborn Collection, Osborn c35.

Ah! Beauteous Nymph, whoe'er thou art,
Who shalt peruse this hapless virgin's Tale,
When pleasure warms thy gentle heart,
By fancy led, & fann'd by rapture's gale,
Expand thy mind – receive the proffered Joy:
The fruit of genuine wit can never cloy.
If tears of sympathy should flow,
Check not the Symptoms of a generous mind:
Who hears, unmoved, another's woe,
No soothing friend in misery shall find.
The pitying bosom claims a sweet relief,
When virtue lulls to ease the social grief.
Deep grave the moral on thy breast,
See saintlike innocence superiour rise,
See Fashion's gaudy slaves deprest,
See, and those lures of Idleness despise,
So, to distinguished Joys thou may'st aspire,
An *Orville* love thee, & the world admire.

Given the dating of October 1778, it seems likely that the Harvard version reproduces a text composed in Shinfield and sent to Frances following Charles's first reading of *Evelina*; this fits with his 1779 reference to 'the little sonnet, *which I gave you some time since*' [italics mine]. This version was probably copied by Charlotte into her miscellany at a much later date, given her attribution of the ecclesiastical title 'D.D.', which Charles only gained in 1812. The Yale version, dated April 1779, probably reflects a process of revision undertaken around the time that Charles was lending *Evelina* around Aberdeen, though its transcription may also have come later.

The two versions are similar, but there are some variations. In April 1779, Charles altered the title so that the poem was 'Addressed to the Ladies' and introduced a more formal, numbered stanzaic arrangement. In line 3, he changed 'Pleasure warm[ing]' the gentle heart to 'pleasure fir[ing]' it. In line 8, he altered 'symptoms of joy' to 'offspring', and in line 11 he refers to the 'tender' rather than 'the pitying' bosom. In line 12, he describes virtue lulling the social grief to 'ease' rather than 'rest'. 'Deep grave the Moral on thy breast' becomes 'O grave the moral on thy heart' and 'Fashion's gaudy slaves depart' is now 'Fashion's glittering slaves deprest'. The most significant difference lies in the last line. Where in October 1778 the poet expresses a wish that 'An *Orville* love [the reader], and the world admire', in April 1779, this becomes 'The Virtuous love thee, and the World admire'. These changes have the interesting effect of both sharpening and blunting the sonnet's sexual connotations. On the one hand, the alterations of 'pleasure *warm*[ing]' the gentle heart to 'pleasure *fir*[ing]' it and '*pitying* bosom' to '*tender* bosom' slightly dial up the sublimated sexual undertones (Charles also uses the verb 'fire' in a poem dedicated to Jessy Willox). On the other hand, the allusion to Orville, which codes the concluding wish as at least partially amatory, has been removed.

Despite the dating of the Yale version to April 1779, I cannot be certain that it accurately replicates the text of Charles's circulated sonnet. At a minimum, the title of the circulated version was different from that of both Harvard and Yale copies, since Charles reports 'address[ing] it "*To the Female Reader*!"' We are therefore dealing with a lost text, suspended in a space of possibility between two alternative drafts.

3.1 'Whoe'er Thou Art': Universal Inscription

In evaluating the poem's genre, we find ourselves on only slightly surer ground. It is superficially an instance of what Heather Jackson calls 'a minor poetic genre, the verse inscription . . . a by-product of the exchange of books between friends and associates'.[156] In certain respects – its recording of a personal response to the text and its encouragement of a related engagement in the subsequent reader – Charles's sonnet fits neatly with Jackson's definition. Like his verses on *Sidney Biddulph* or *The Good Natur'd Man*, the sonnet seeks to provide a set of affective parameters within which 'the female reader' should respond to the novel. Both versions are full of imperative instructions – to 'expand thy mind', 'check not the offspring of a generous mind', 'grave the moral', and 'see' the readings that the poet takes of the plot's resolution. The poet presents *Evelina*, decisively, as a sentimental fiction. However, the sonnet does not record 'circumstances of presentation', which Jackson considers a core characteristic of the verse inscription. Neither does it work to 'personalise' the book, an objective which the Multigraph Collective considers its primary function.[157] Charles's inscription is, in fact, strikingly *im*personal, both in its terms of address ('whoe'er thou art') and its infinitely portable positioning (attached – but, we must assume, only temporarily – to a library book which is neither fully the property of the inscriber nor destined to be fully the property of the reader).

At this point, we must remind ourselves that the first recipient of the poem, in 1778, was Frances Burney herself. Granted, the verse does not address her directly, unless we read a tenuous pun into the slightly odd verb 'fann'd'.[158] Charles's intention was probably to have it circulated through the wider family and beyond. Nonetheless, in directing the sonnet through Frances's hands,

---

[156] Jackson *Marginalia*, 67. See also Towsey, *Reading the Scottish Enlightenment*, 175–6.

[157] Multigraph Collective, *Interacting with Print*, 201, 211.

[158] Frances's family nicknames included 'Fan', 'Fanchon', and 'Fannikin', as well as the famous 'Fanny'.

Charles implicitly subordinates her creative work to his own act of critical interpretation. In characterising *Evelina* as a sentimental fiction with a didactic 'moral', he closes off alternative readings (some of which he acknowledges himself, in the Shinfield fragments, with his comic mimicry of Duval and his comparison to Sterne and Fielding). In so doing, he imposes a reading of Frances Burney's authorial character as well as the nature of her production. Moreover, if she is included within the compass of the sonnet's readership, the final couplet reads as a remarkable attempt at gendered constraint. The 'distinguished joys' to which Charles's sister may 'aspire' are not only the admiration of 'the World' (which may be either literary or moral) but also the love of a man like Lord Orville, and presumably the domestic role of wifehood that must follow. In the Harvard version, then, there is an attempt on Charles's part to contain, even as he compliments, the scope of his sister's achievement.

The amendments of April 1779, especially the new title, slightly alter the poem's tenor. I discuss these amendments fully in Section 5, in which I evaluate Charles's (lack of) success in using his inscription to construct a reading community in which his poetic offerings might generate amatory, and subsequently material, advantage. I now turn to consider the likely physical positioning of the lost sonnet in the Aberdeen *Evelina*.

3.2 The 'Prefixed' Poem as Paratext

What are the implications of the word 'prefix', with which Charles describes the physical positioning of his manuscript sonnet in relation to his sister's printed text? What Abigail Williams gracefully calls the 'unmatchable portability' of verse inscription presents several possibilities.[159] Charles might have written directly on a page or pastedown. Alternatively, he might have written on a loose sheet of paper, which he attached to the volume using an adhesive. Finally, he might have simply tucked such a sheet between two pages. The title of the Yale version indicates that the sonnet was 'written in Evelina' and the title of the Harvard version suggests that it was 'written in a blank leaf of Evelina', but unfortunately we cannot draw any solid inference from such claims, since, as Jackson notes, the poetic conceit that verses were inscribed *in* a book should not necessarily be taken literally.[160] Neither is Samuel Johnson's *Dictionary* much help in narrowing the options: he defines the verb 'prefix' as simply 'to put before another thing' with no remark as to the mode or permanency of the placing.[161]

We must turn, then, to the layout of early editions of *Evelina* to ascertain where Charles's poem might have been placed and how a reader might have

---

[159] Williams, *The Social Life of Books*, 128.   [160] Jackson, *Marginalia,* 67.
[161] Johnson, *Dictionary*.

experienced it. As it happens, Lowndes's first three printings of *Evelina* are all very similar in their structural layout. There are three places where the sonnet might credibly have been placed so that it would satisfy Charles's description, Johnson's definition, and the implications of the various titles. The first possibility is the pastedown inside the front cover of the first volume, which was where Charles glued his bookplate in the books he stole in Cambridge (see Section 5, particularly Figures 13 and 14). The second is the blank verso preceding the title page of the first volume. In the Aberdeen edition, a set of unusual markings suggest that significant activity has taken place in this space (see Figure 2). The pitted residue suggests that something may have been pasted on this verso and then removed (see Figures 13 and 14 for similar markings in the Cambridge volumes), while the smears on the title page itself suggest the smudging of wet ink when the volume was peremptorily closed. (If this is indeed the Banff *Evelina*, and if we take the markings to mean that a loose sheet was pasted onto the flyleaf, then it would follow that Charles applied his prefixing practice to the Banff copy as well as the Aberdeen one.) The third possibility is that Charles's sonnet was placed not on the pastedown or the blank verso facing the title page but on the following one: the reverse of the title page itself. In first, second, and third editions, this blank leaf faces Frances's own dedicatory ode to her father, 'To -------- ---------' (see Figure 8). The fact that placing the poem after the title page would slightly less precisely fulfil Johnson's definition of 'put[ting] before', combined with the lack of any similar traces of pasting or writing in the SC *Evelina*, makes this the least likely eventuality in my view.

Placement in any of these locations raises the possibility that, notwithstanding its manuscript character, a reader might experience Charles's sonnet as a prefatory piece of paratext. Such a claim takes a disruptive approach to the long-standing formal definition of paratextuality, which presumes a degree of legitimation by the author.[162] However, this presumption seems to me unnecessarily constrictive. In privileging an authorial perspective over a reader-centred one, we risk dangerously overstating the author's role in the publication process. In fact, as Svetlana Kochkina has shown, Frances Burney had negligible control over many paratextual aspects of her work: the title, attribution, illustrations, and advertisements were all entirely within the publisher's remit. Indeed, in the case of foreign editions, some publishers saw nothing wrong with inserting newly commissioned prefaces, removing Burney's own peritexts, or even truncating the

---

[162] Gérard Genette defines the paratext as 'the conveyor of a commentary that is authorial or more or less legitimated by the author'. See Genette, *Paratexts*, 2, and Readioff, 'Recent Approaches', 3.

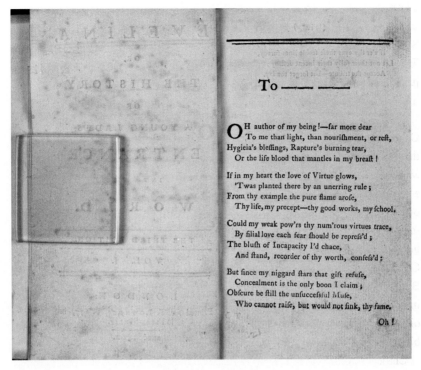

Figure 8 Prefatory ode.
Frances Burney, *Evelina, or, the History of a Young Lady's Entrance into the World*
(London: Lowndes, third edition, 1779), vol. 1, unpaginated. Aberdeen, University of
Aberdeen, SB 82366 E1.

text itself.[163] Moreover, in permitting authorial sanction to define paratext,
we lose the opportunity to fully illuminate effects of embellished texts
whose contemporary readerships had a much greater familiarity with hybrid
manuscript-print culture than our own. As Betty Schellenberg has shown,
'media of script and print, [despite] their distinctive practices and priorities,
were in close conversation' in late eighteenth-century literary culture.[164]
The Multigraph Collective goes further, asserting that serious consideration
of 'manuscript-print hybrids' is a core component of its headline enterprise
to 'restore ... [print culture] to the media ecology in which it was historic-
ally embedded'.[165] Since Charles evidently advertised his close relationship
to the author of *Evelina* so openly, the effect on a reader of his sonnet's
placement at the beginning of her book might well be to establish him as
a legitimated editorial presence. Such an act would contribute towards

---

[163] Kochkina, *Frances Burney's* Evelina, 178–180.   [164] Schellenberg, *Literary Coteries*, 2.
[165] Multigraph Collective, *Interacting with Print,* 186, 10.

Charles's effort to promote himself as an accomplished young poet and belletrist who was an active member of a celebrated literary dynasty. In Section 5, I consider more fully how Charles emphasised his kinship with Frances, occasionally against her wishes, to achieve this effect. The material juxtaposition of their literary endeavours, via his 'prefixed' sonnet, is an important part of this enterprise.

However, in positioning his poem directly or shortly before Frances's ode, Charles is perhaps also doing something more instinctive – and less cynical – than advertising his celebrity connections or exploiting his sister's achievement. Many scholars, following Margaret Doody's example, have adopted a psychoanalytic approach to Frances Burney's writings – and the prefatory ode that opens *Evelina* is a prime candidate for such an enterprise.[166] If, with them, we read it as a vehicle within which Frances attempts to reconcile filial humility with authorly ambition, then there is something poignant about Charles's cognate attempt, at a moment when he was 'Torn from my Father, Brothers, Sisters, Friend' (as he put it in one of his poems),[167] to insert himself into the ode's orbit alongside his father and sister. *Evelina's* paratextual threshold provides a site upon which Charles attempts to reunite the family unit that his crime has rent asunder.

Charles's ability to reunite himself with his family is enhanced by his choice of form. Though generally famed for their prose creations, all members of the Burney family were prolific poets, and this aspect of their creative practice is beginning to receive welcome attention.[168] The composition of verse was one crucial way in which they expressed affection, marked occasions, and curated an archive for their own pleasure and that of posterity. This enterprise was spearheaded by Dr Burney himself, who wrote hundreds of occasional verses for family and friends during his lifetime. Frances's decision to address her father in verse can be read as an acknowledgement of the importance of form in currying filial favour. Conscious of the risks of her fictional enterprise in the pages that follow, her deferential ode eases the transition towards her declaration of formal independence.

As we have seen, Charles defines himself primarily as a poet during his time in Aberdeen, at a time when a prosaic and scholarly self-fashioning would have made more sense for his future career. We might read his alienated versification, including his poetic occupation of blank space in Frances's book, as a literary performance in partial emulation of both his father and his sister. In affective terms, this is a complex act, which includes a note of appropriation. In the astute

---

[166] Doody, *The Life in the Works,* 31–32.
[167] Charles Burney, 'Verse Letter to F.J.H.W', OSB MSS 3, Box 7, Folder 480.
[168] Clark, 'Growing Up Burney', Bander, 'The Astronomical Muse'.

words of the Multigraph Collective, 'tipped-in materials threaten to disrupt or even swallow up the printed text, raising questions about its primacy'.[169] In Shinfield in 1778, two of Charles's earliest responses to *Evelina* had been a pedantic correction to the grammar of Frances's ode and a sonnet attempting to control her reading of her own novel. In Aberdeen, we find him forcibly inserting his own literary production into her text – 'a violent form of inter-activity', especially given the oft-drawn parallels, in contemporary and modern discussions of textuality, between print codex and corporeal body.[170] His sonnet inscription expresses, in Jackson's words, 'the primary impulse of claiming the book as one's own'.[171] A similar note of appropriation is evident in the contemporary letter to Frances, in which Charles cannot resist hinting that his circulated poetry receives similar acclaim to her prose: '*That* likewise had its *admirers*'.[172]

4 Reading *Evelina*

The theory that Frances Burney may have based the character of Macartney on Charles is almost as old as *Evelina* itself. According to Hester Thrale, Frances Crewe Greville (1748–1818) asked her:

> if the Story in Fanny Burney's Book – Evelina – about Mr Macartney was not founded on Fact, for said She I had heard it was true, and that She had told you so; and that you had told many, how the Anecdote or Circumstance or what you will of Macartney's going to shoot himself actually did happen to her own Brother Charles Burney, who having been expelled by the University & forbidden his Fathers house was actually discovered by his Sister Fanny in the desperate State mentioned of Macartney.[173]

However, Thrale does not confirm the rumour, and, as Doody points out, the chronology of Evelina's composition makes the suggested process impossible. Macartney's attempted suicide takes place midway through the second volume, which by January 1777 – some nine months before Charles's disgrace – Frances had finished and sent to Lowndes.[174] Nonetheless, the rumour has proved irresistible to biographers: Kate Chisholm speculates that Frances returned to her manuscript to 'embellish' her character of Macartney 'after witnessing such scenes with Charles'.[175]

It is undeniable that there are striking parallels between Macartney and Charles, which extend well beyond the fraternal relationship to Evelina/

[169] Multigraph Collective, *Interacting with Print*, 289.
[170] Multigraph Collective, *Interacting with Print*, 210.   [171] Jackson, *Marginalia*, 90.
[172] Charles Burney to Frances Burney, OSB MSS 3, Box 6, Folder 381.
[173] Hester Thrale Piozzi, 18 Jan. 1779, in Balderston, *Thraliana*, 1:360.
[174] Doody, *The Life in the Works*, 61.   [175] Chisholm, *Fanny Burney*, 54.

Frances. Though Macartney is Scottish by birth and Charles only by residence, both 'finish [their] education' in Aberdeen. They are both 'designed for the church'. Then there is the 'rashness' of disposition and the 'misery' of circumstance. Finally, there is the 'poetical turn' common to both, which often manifests in a tone of courtly eroticism, blurring the line between fraternal and amatory affections.[176] Here, I suggest, inverting the logic of Chisholm and others, that life may have mirrored art. Rather than Frances basing her character on her brother, Charles's poetic style and his patterns of literary sociability were inspired by his reading of Macartney.

At this point, a brief review of Macartney's role within the plot might be useful. Evelina first encounters him when she makes a visit to her vulgar mercantile cousins, the Branghtons, in whose upper rooms he lodges. He is introduced as 'a young man, in deep mourning ... apparently in profound and melancholy meditation'.[177] Upon Evelina's enquiry, Miss Branghton dismisses him as 'nothing but a poor Scotch poet!' This is confirmed when Evelina subsequently overhears Macartney reciting his own composition, a 'harsh' set of meditations on 'LIFE!' which she deems indicative of an effecting 'internal wretchedness'.[178] The 'rashness and the misery' of 'this ill-fated young man' continue to 'engross all [her] thoughts' until she catches him planning to take his own life.[179] Having removed his pistols and averted his suicide attempt, Evelina offers Macartney money to support himself, which he gratefully accepts.[180] Her generosity inspires his admiration and devotion, expressed through the courtly poetry he circulates in her praise and his reiterated request for private meetings, which cause misunderstandings on the part of Lord Orville.[181] All suspicions are laid to rest, however, when Macartney and Evelina are revealed to share a father in the errant Sir John Belmont.[182] When the confusion has been cleared up, a double marriage takes place between Lord Orville and Evelina, and Macartney and Polly Green – who has passed, through no fault of her own, as the daughter of Sir John Belmont.[183] By the end of the novel, Macartney's circumstances have improved markedly, thanks to his poetic skill and ability to inspire pity in his sympathetic sister-benefactress. He is reconciled with his lost family and makes what will surely be – given Orville's insistence that Evelina and Polly are treated as co-heiresses to the Belmont fortune – a highly advantageous marriage.

At a moment when Charles felt alienated from his family and entertained many justified fears about his future prospects, I think it likely that Macartney's fictional trajectory offered him opportunities for optimistic identification. Crucially, Macartney goes from rags to riches via his poetic endeavours,

---

[176] Burney, *Evelina*, 227, 186, 335.   [177] Burney, *Evelina*, 177.
[178] Burney, *Evelina*, 178–179.   [179] Burney, *Evelina*, 186.   [180] Burney, *Evelina*, 207.
[181] Burney, *Evelina*, 333.   [182] Burney, *Evelina*, 321.   [183] Burney, *Evelina*, 404.

which stimulate Evelina's admiration and pity, and ultimately inspire her to offer financial patronage. Such an example might explain Charles's propensity during this period for certain modes of suppliant positioning, evidence of which survives in the social verse he circulated to genteel young women. It might also explain his textual attempts to offer Frances's narrative as an instructive parable to those potential patrons whose hearts might be softened by his uncertain situation and poetic acumen, as well as by his sister's skill. Finally, it might account for his insistent conflation of Frances herself with the character of Evelina – which logic, followed to its natural conclusion, would position her brother as Macartney.

4.1 The 'Poetical Turn'

A close reading of Charles's manuscript poetry offers further evidence for this theory. As I noted in Section 1, early 1778 marks a distinct shift in Charles's poetic practice as he transitions from writing comic light verse to earnest neo-classical odes. I think it likely that such a shift was a consequence of reading *Evelina* (which the correspondence suggests he was doing at that time) and emulating Macartney's poetic style – which was, of course, really Frances's own.

Macartney's first poem is the doleful 'fragment of an ode' beginning 'O LIFE!' This 'tortured outpouring of sensibility', which scholars have compared to the works of Thomas Grey, Charles Cotton, and Abraham Cowley, hints at past and present sufferings, and reflects on the mutability of life, a 'gilded, but a bitter pill / Of varied, great, and complicated ill!'[184] Charles's verse 'Letter to F.J.H.W.', addressed to his friend Francis Wollaston and dated 3 February 1778, takes a similarly gloomy tone to Macartney's, bemoaning that in the 'bowl of bliss ... which Fate prepares / The bitter ever mingles with the sweet! / No certain happiness this life can bring! / We all must taste Misfortune's nauseous Spring'. Where Macartney characterises life as a 'lingering dream', 'flattering with Hope most fair', Charles calls 'flattering Hope' an illusion, replaced by an 'empty dream'. Macartney characterises life's progress as pursued by 'Mis'ry', whereas Charles refers to himself as 'to misery a prey'.[185] Such insistent semantic echoes indicate a relationship between the two poems, although the precise nature of that relationship must remain uncertain.

Soon after reading *Evelina*, Charles also started, like Macartney, writing courtly poems to young ladies. These verses strongly resemble the second work by Macartney quoted within Frances's narrative: the verses on Evelina dropped in the pump room.

---

[184] Burney, *Evelina*, n.179; Whitehead, 'A Various Complicated Ill'.
[185] 'A Verse Letter to F.J.H.W.', OSB MSS 3, Box 7, Folder 480.

See last advance, with bashful grace,
Downcast eye, and blushing cheek,
Timid air, and beauteous face,
Anville, – whom the Graces seek.

Though ev'ry beauty is her own,
And though her mind each virtue fills,
Anville, – to her power unknown,
Artless, strikes, – unconscious, kills![186]

Gallant verse is heavily conventional by nature, but Charles's 'Ode [addressed to Nancy Gordon]' and 'Ode addressed to Miss Rachel and Miss Jessy Willox' display particularly strong similarities to this fragment. Like Macartney's poem, both odes affect the conceit that the young ladies appear in a procession of beauties over whom they ultimately claim pre-eminence (the first lines, respectively, are 'See Nancy comes, like Beauty's queen' and 'They come! Adorn'd with every grace').[187] Both, like Macartney's poem, showcase familiarity with classical tropes in their references to the Graces, and play heavily on the (somewhat didactic) tension between physical beauty and moral virtue. Both date to the spring of 1779: precisely the time when Charles was lending the novel to Jessy, Rachel, and Nancy in turn.

4.2 Sisters, lovers, and patrons

Many scholars have noted Macartney's uneasy position in Frances Burney's narrative, poised between the roles of prospective lover and brother. Such observations are far from new. The potential erotics of Macartney's relationship to Evelina are clearly marked in visual depictions of the characters produced and circulated in the 1780s and 1790s, all of which depict the averted suicide attempt. The earliest (aside from an illustration by Burney's cousin Edward Francisco, now lost) is an engraving by Nicolas Colibert, printed in London in 1786, in which Evelina accosts Macartney kneeling in his bedchamber (see Figure 9). As Burney's narrative specifies, he has fallen to his knees and points a pair of pistols to his breast and throat. Evelina, having caught his arm, points to the heavens, presumably to reproach him for his sin. Macartney's face is on a level with, and rather close to, Evelina's exposed décolletage. While the only piece of furniture mentioned in Burney's narrative is a table, Colibert has placed a rumpled bed prominently in the left side of the background. The casts of Macartney and Evelina's faces are similar, marking them out as brother and sister: but the positioning of the figures and choice of furniture indicate an

---

[186] Burney, *Evelina*, 333.   [187] Osborn c38, 12–13 and 28–29.

Figure 9 Nicolas Colibert, 'Evelina surprising Mr Macartney preparing to load his pistols'.
Stipple engraving (London: William Dickinson, 1786). London, British Museum, 1897,1117.222. © The Trustees of the British Museum.

uneasy awareness of their physical proximity, heightened emotions, and liminal relationship.

Visual representations of the Evelina/Macartney relationship become more emphatically erotic if we allow ourselves to glance, momentarily, beyond British borders. As Antoinette Sol, Martha J. Koehler and Svetlana Kochkina have all shown, Burney's early novels were popular in France, where they were often appropriated to culturally or politically radical usages. Where Sol and Koehler suggest that *Evelina* is an important thematic and stylistic model for

Choderlos de Laclos's scandalous novel *Les Liaisons Dangereuses*,[188] Kochkina argues that illustrative frontispieces for French translations of Burney's novel evolved, during the 1790s, to subtly signal adherence to revolutionary principles.[189] This broad pattern of transgressive translation is evident in extant French images of Macartney's suicide attempt. See, for example, an illustration (Figure 10) which opens the first volume of a 1795 edition published in Paris by Pierre-Sebastien Leprieur. Like Colibert, Leprieur's illustrator has made Macartney's bed a key feature of the scene. But they have also gone further in presenting *Evelina* lying prone on the floor, her eyes closed, and her arms thrown open invitingly. Macartney kneels over her, his own arms spread to mirror her positioning. The caption reads, 'J'ai saisi son bras, et suis tombée moi-même, sans connaissance', highlighting the moment, immediately after preventing Macartney from shooting himself, when Evelina faints – and presumably inviting the reader to speculate about what may have happened during her loss of consciousness. Another French edition published three years later by Jean-Baptiste Imbert replicates Leprieur's interpretation of the scene almost exactly (see Figure 11). In this rendition, Evelina is clearly conscious, but her positioning is even more suggestive. The angle of her legs suggests an entanglement with Macartney's own. She is gripping his wrist, and he is about to clasp hers in reciprocation, in a manner that reinforces physical contact between the two while the bed looms over them.

The contemporary erotic resonance of the Macartney–Evelina relationship can help to account for some of the more puzzling elements of Charles's reader responses. If we accept that he started to identify as Macartney in Shinfield, sending his courtly sonnet to his sister would make far more sense as a performance of that identity. The following year, his insertion of his own poetic contribution into the body of her book would indicate another performance of this liminal fraternal-erotic role.

If Charles's performance of Macartney induced him to treat his sister like a lover, the converse is also true, since his amorous approaches to young women in Aberdeen are oddly formatted as intense expressions of fraternal affection. In particular, his poems addressed to Rachel and Jessy Willox muddle amorous language with kinship terminology. He frequently addresses them as 'the *Sisters*'[190] and draws attention to the qualities they share with Frances and Susanna: 'My own dear Fanny & Susan excepted, I must confess I never saw the two Girls, whom I doated upon with such ardent admiration.'[191]

---

[188] Sol, *Textual Promiscuities*; Koehler, *Models of Reading*.
[189] Kochkina, *Frances Burney's Evelina*, 41.
[190] 'Ode, addressed to Miss Rachel, and Jessy Willox', Osborn c38.
[191] Charles Burney to Frances Burney [Feb/ March 1780], OSB MSS 3, Box 6, Folder 427.

Figure 10 Illustrative frontispiece to 1795 French edition of *Evelina*.
Evelina, Roman: Nouvellement traduit et rédigé avec beaucoup de soin d'aprés
l'Anglois de MISS BURNEY (Paris: Leprieur, l'an IV de la République franç.), vol. 1,
unpaginated. Montreal, McGill University Library, Rare Books and Special Collections,
OCTAVO-398.

When he remarks their similarities to Richardson's Charlotte Grandison and Lady
L, he tellingly casts them as the hero's sisters rather than his love interests. Such
choices suggest that Charles not only positioned himself as a gallant suppliant for
patronage to the Willox sisters in the same manner as Macartney does to Evelina
but also implicitly placed his relationship towards them along similar axes of
brother/lover.

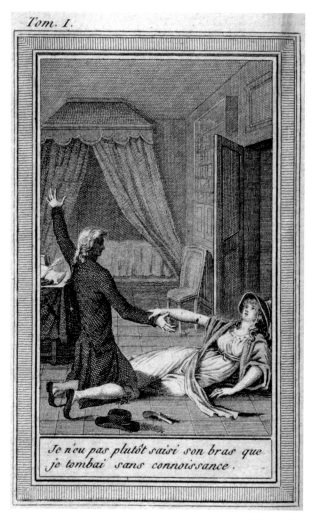

Tom. I.

Je n'eu pas plutôt saisi son bras que je tombai sans connoissance.

Figure 11 Illustrative frontispiece to 1798 French edition of *Evelina*. *Evelina. ou, l'entrée d'une jeune personne dans le monde. Par Miss Burney, traduit de l'Anglais.* (Paris: Imbert, 1798.), vol. 1, unpaginated. Montreal, McGill University Library, Rare Books and Special Collections, PR3316 A4 E814 1798b.

Charles's identified performance of Macartney can be characterised as an act of readerly poaching. In it, we can detect not only the process of textual 'detach-[ment]' outlined by de Certeau but also a loss of grasp on 'fictive securities of reality'.[192] Crucially, I believe that Charles is no isolated case in this respect, and that such activity took place within a broader culture of identified performance in response to Frances Burney's fiction. Next, I briefly consider some other reader

---

[192] Certeau, *The Practice of Everyday Life*, 133, 135.

testimonies which hint at the ability of Frances Burney's fiction to render the boundary between text and reality porous, and consider the implications for gendered models of reading in circulation at the time.

4.3 The Poaching Economy

'[B]y some other removals, and a little scheming of her own, Anne was enabled to place herself much nearer the end of the bench than she had been before, much more within reach of a passer-by. She could not do so, without comparing herself with Miss Larolles, the inimitable Miss Larolles; but still she did it.'[193]

At this moment in Jane Austen's *Persuasion*, Anne Elliott finds herself inching towards the end of a row of auditors at a concert, hoping that such a position will give Frederick Wentworth easy access should he wish to strike up a conversation. Anne sheepishly contemplates the similarities between her own behaviour and that of Frances Burney's character Miss Larolles, who, in her second novel *Cecilia*, 'sat at the outside on purpose to speak to a person or two [the fop Mr Meadows], that I knew would be strolling about'.[194] Making the patient, self-effacing Anne align herself with the scheming, coquettish Larolles is a superb stroke of comedy on Austen's part, which coaxes the reader to acknowledge and appreciate this most reserved heroine's surprising ability to laugh at herself. It also acts as a critical comment on Burney's unique capacities as a novelist which is quite as complimentary as, though more subtle than, Austen's more famous references to her work scattered throughout *Northanger Abbey*.[195] The word 'inimitable' must be read ironically, since imitating Larolles is precisely what Anne finds herself doing. And she is far from alone. Anne Elliott's fictional imitation and Charles Burney's real identified performance take place within a broader poaching economy.

Reader identification has generated much insightful scholarship in eighteenth-century studies over recent decades. Frances Burney is often one of the key novelists employed in this enterprise, since she records dozens of cases, in her *Journals and Letters*, of readers identifying, feeling with, and fantasising about her creations. There has been a particularly rich seam of scholarship interrogating the relation between identification and performance in reader interactions with Burney's characters. Patricia Michaelson, Francesca Saggini, Abigail Williams, and Jan Fergus have all exploited Burney family accounts of reading aloud – often Frances' own novels or plays – suggesting that such sessions might have 'imitated the rhetorical and performance conventions employed by actors on stage' and 'enabled alternative forms of engagement with fictional works in which the

---

[193] Austen, *Persuasion*, 153.   [194] Sabor and Doody, *Cecilia*, 286.
[195] Halsey, *Jane Austen and Her Readers*, 58.

relationship between reader and character could be seen as a matter of performance rather than immersion'.[196]

My reading of Charles's identified performance as Macartney strikes out from such scholarship in two ways. I exploit Charles's poetic archive, rather than his prose life writing, as the main primary source, and embellish it with bibliographic analysis of the surviving traces of his bookish activity. Such 3D reading, as I indicate in my Introduction, can give us evidence of reader responses that to some extent short-circuit the problem of unreliability inherent in a self-conscious account of reading practice. Furthermore, I deploy a range of such traces made over an extended period – in this case, three years. Sustained echoes of a character's manner, behaviour, and register suggest that Frances Burney's characters provoke sustained performances: those which are not confined to closed reading sessions, but rather adopted as shapers of everyday textual and verbal behaviours, enabling the performer to blur the boundary between fiction and reality in their everyday life. In short, I am interested in real-life quixotes.

Contemporary anxieties about the tendency of eighteenth-century sentimental fiction to stimulate quixotism in young female readers have often been remarked.[197] Frances Burney's novels, however, have seldom been considered within the compass of such anxiety, partly because scholars have swallowed wholesale Burney's own insistence, first pitched in her *Address to the Critics* preceding *Evelina* and frequently reiterated in her life writing, that her novels should be read within the masculine literary tradition of Richardson and Fielding rather than the female-profiled 'romance'. However, ample evidence exists that they *did* generate such anxiety among a contemporary readership. Hannah More, in a little-known letter to her friend Mary Hamilton (1756–1816), reported the view of Queen Charlotte – which apparently dovetailed with her own – that Evelina and Cecilia were insufficiently pious to act as positive role models: 'Miss Burney's heroines wou'd certainly be much better women, and brighter patterns, if their pure morals were perfected by piety, and if in their distresses they looked for help where only it is to be found.'[198] A young Maria Edgeworth had a different, but related, objection:

> Why then did Miss Burney give [Lord Orville] a title? was it to recommend him to title Readers? If so she did either their Taste, or her Book, great Injustice – And, (if I may be so bold to say <it>) her young female *Plebeian* admirers some Injury – for I cannot help thinking that raising their hopes & Expectations above, what in the ordinary course of things they

[196] Saggini, *Backstage in the Novel*, 5; Williams, *The Social Life of Books*, 72, 221–222.
[197] Williams, *The Social Life of Books*, 211; Halsey, *Jane Austen and Her Readers*, 30–35 and 119–134; de Ritter *Imagining Women Readers,* 17–21.
[198] Hannah More to Mary Hamilton, 30 October 1782, Houghton, MS Eng 1778 116.

are likely to attain, *is* doing them an injury – It is preparing for them Disappointment & Ennui at least – Evelina had no title & but small Fortune, but she married an Earl! – Will no conclusions be drawn from this? will no hopes be raised? Can an improbable event be brought about by probable means, without lessening our Opinion of its probability? – Even connecting the idea of every thing that is amiable in a Husband with the ideas of a Lord & a Coronet is, I should think, hurtful – But perhaps Miss Burney had reasons to counterbalance these which have not occurred to me.[199]

There is a certain irony to Edgeworth's concern about young *female* readers identifying with unrealistic marital ambitions, since the only actual example I have found of an impressionable young 'reader' forming unrealistic conjugal aspirations after reading *Evelina* is that of Charles Burney himself. His dogged pursuit of the Willox sisters (and possibly later Jane Abernethie), via poetic performances suggesting intensive identification with Macartney, offers evidence of the effects of a masculine sensibility which, steeped in theatrical performance and literary tropes, could find it difficult to distinguish fiction from reality.

In one of the most important studies of eighteenth-century readership, Jan Fergus elegantly demonstrates how historical and literary methodologies can complement one another, using *Evelina* as a case study. Building on the discovery that eighteenth-century men actually borrowed more novels than women, Fergus implores scholars to 'ask more insistently how men positioned themselves when they read novels, ... [to] more closely examine what male fantasies are exercised and satisfied by these works ... [to] look at so-called 'women's novels' with an eye to how they construct men and male reading'.[200] Fergus's perceptive but fleeting example is that of Frances Burney's father, Dr Charles Burney, 'reading himself into' the paternalistic clergyman Mr Villars in *Evelina* when, according to his daughter Susan, he declares, 'That man is ALWAYS right!'[201]

In recent years, we have had no shortage of studies dissecting the quixotic reader as a literary device.[202] Conversely – unless we are content to make do with the old rumours about Goethe's *Sorrows of Young Werther* (1774) triggering a spate of deaths by suicide – there is still a real paucity of scholarship exploring actual documented cases of over-identification. Fergus proposes that we look for quixotes not only in the pages of novels but also in manuscript life writing – and that we prioritise for analysis those 'male fantasies' that were inspired, fulfilled, or satirised by sentimental (often female-authored) fictions. The younger Charles Burney's performance of Macartney offers a rare

---

[199] Maria Edgeworth to Fanny Robinson, 15 August [1783], qtd. in Havens, 'Maria Edgeworth's [Deleted] Thoughts'.
[200] Fergus, *Provincial Readers*, 73–74. [201] Fergus, *Provincial Readers*, 74.
[202] Dale, 'The Quixotic Eighteenth Century'.

opportunity to do so, while adding to the body of scholarship showing that sentimental novels written by women were popular among, and exercised a powerful influence upon, male readers.[203] Illustrative frontispieces and prints, letters, and poetry deployed in this section illuminate some of the 'male fantasies' that *Evelina* exercised and satisfied. In the next and final section, I evaluate Charles's (lack of) success in realising his aspirations.

5 Loaning *Evelina*

At this point, I must state clearly one fact which is crucial to my argument. In the late 1770s and early 1780s, Charles Burney could not afford to buy his own books. It is sometimes forgotten, given their social connections and extraordinary achievements, that the Burneys were far from a wealthy family – a 'very low race of Mortals', as Hester Thrale once reflected[204] – whose close relatives were coffee shop proprietors, milliners, pawnbrokers, and odd-job men.[205] By Charles's own account, later verified by Frances, during his student years, he received an allowance from his father which was much more 'scanty' than those of his peers.[206] Nine-shilling books, therefore, would have been a luxury commodity that he could not afford.[207] Such financial precarity made him a borrower in formal and informal loan economies by necessity rather than choice. In this section, I take a closer look at how membership of Alexander Angus's circulating library in Aberdeen was prescribed and practiced, and how it shaped Charles's own practice as lender, prefixer, and reader.

5.1 'The Custody of the Subscriber': Borrowing *Evelina*

As noted in Section 2, I cannot be certain that Angus's was the institution where Charles obtained the Aberdeen *Evelina*. However, as 'the leading bookshop in the north-east of Scotland' and 'one of the most complete libraries of any type in

---

[203] Sol, *Textual Promiscuities*; Koehler, *Models of Reading*; Lynch, *Loving Literature*. According to the *Books and Borrowing* database, Frances Burney's novels were borrowed from Scottish libraries 420 times before 1830; only 28 borrowers are female, whereas 392 are male. See *Books and Borrowing: An Analysis of Scottish Borrowers' Registers, 1750–1830*, s.v., "Simple search for 'Author forename: Frances, Author surname: Burney'," accessed 27 February 2024, https://borrowing.stir.ac.uk/search/p-1/0/0/simple/afname|Frances/asname|Burney.

[204] *Thraliana* 1:368, n.3.

[205] One of Robert Burnside's letters to Charles (27 August 1781, OSB MSS 3, Box 3, Folder 158) is addressed to 'Mr Sleepe's, PawnBroker, Watford'. This must have been one of Charles's maternal uncles: Richard Sleepe, Francis Sleepe, or Joshua Sleepe. For other lesser-known Burney and Sleepe occupations, see Erickson, 'Esther Sleepe'. For an early acknowledgement of the family's general economic precarity, see Gallagher, *Nobody's Story*, Chapter 5.

[206] Frances Burney to Charles Parr Burney, 26 February 1818, *JL* 10:795. See also Walker, 'Charles Burney's Theft', 323–324.

[207] Williams, *The Social Life of Books*, 98–9.

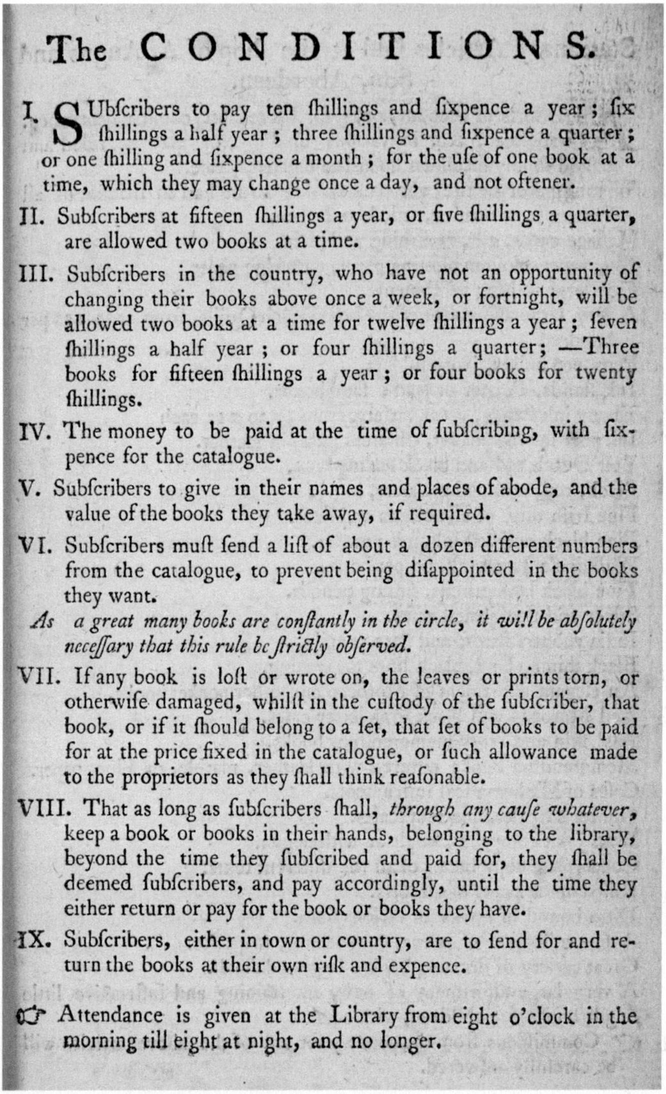

The CONDITIONS.

I. SUbscribers to pay ten shillings and sixpence a year; six shillings a half year; three shillings and sixpence a quarter; or one shilling and sixpence a month; for the use of one book at a time, which they may change once a day, and not oftener.

II. Subscribers at fifteen shillings a year, or five shillings a quarter, are allowed two books at a time.

III. Subscribers in the country, who have not an opportunity of changing their books above once a week, or fortnight, will be allowed two books at a time for twelve shillings a year; seven shillings a half year; or four shillings a quarter; —Three books for fifteen shillings a year; or four books for twenty shillings.

IV. The money to be paid at the time of subscribing, with sixpence for the catalogue.

V. Subscribers to give in their names and places of abode, and the value of the books they take away, if required.

VI. Subscribers must send a list of about a dozen different numbers from the catalogue, to prevent being disappointed in the books they want.
As a great many books are constantly in the circle, it will be absolutely necessary that this rule be strictly observed.

VII. If any book is lost or wrote on, the leaves or prints torn, or otherwise damaged, whilst in the custody of the subscriber, that book, or if it should belong to a set, that set of books to be paid for at the price fixed in the catalogue, or such allowance made to the proprietors as they shall think reasonable.

VIII. That as long as subscribers shall, *through any cause whatever,* keep a book or books in their hands, belonging to the library, beyond the time they subscribed and paid for, they shall be deemed subscribers, and pay accordingly, until the time they either return or pay for the book or books they have.

IX. Subscribers, either in town or country, are to send for and return the books at their own risk and expence.

☞ Attendance is given at the Library from eight o'clock in the morning till eight at night, and no longer.

Figure 12 Alexander Angus's *Conditions*.
Appendix to *A New Catalogue of the Aberdeen Circulating Library,* 1779, unpaginated.
Aberdeen, University of Aberdeen, (SC) SBL 1779 NP 2.

the entire country' which, we know, held Frances Burney's *Evelina* in 1779, it has a decent chance of being his source.[208] In any case, the survival of a rare copy of its *Conditions* of membership (see Figure 12), fortuitously dated to the

---

[208] McDonald, 'Circulating Libraries', 120; Towsey, *Reading the Scottish Enlightenment,* 111; Stewart-Murphy, *A History of British Circulating Libraries*, Plate II, unpaginated. The *Books and Borrowing* database finds *Evelina* in only one other Scottish library before 1786 (the St. Andrews' University Library).

very year that Charles borrowed *Evelina*, gives a valuable instance of the general ethos of an Aberdeen circulating library at this time, which can fruitfully be mapped against Charles's documented practice.

Among other things, the *Conditions* provide valuable information about the implicit contract which Angus expected his subscribers to observe, including several behaviours which would incur a financial penalty.

> *VII. If any book is lost or wrote on, the leaves or prints torn, or otherwise damaged, whilst in the custody of the subscriber, that book, or if it should belong to a set, that set of books to be paid for at the price fixed in the catalogue, or such allowance made to the proprietors as they shall think reasonable.*
>
> *VIII. That as long as subscribers shall, through any cause whatever, keep a book or books in their hands, belonging to the library, beyond the time they subscribed and paid for, they shall be deemed subscribers, and pay accordingly, until the time they either return or pay for the book or books they have.*

It is difficult to judge how seriously such delinquencies were taken in practice. One must imagine that overdue loans, then as now, were a common phenomenon, and that only a small financial penalty was imposed for a small infraction.[209] The caveat 'or such allowance made to the proprietors as they shall think reasonable' suggests that there was also room for negotiation when it came to minor markings. With respect to deliberately unreturned books and unresponsive borrowers, however, circulating library proprietors could apparently take recovery quite seriously. Devendra Varma points to a newspaper advertisement placed in 1795 by one circulating library proprietor appealing for assistance in tracing unreturned books, and promising 'an ample Reward . . . on conviction of the offenders'.[210]

Mindful of Charles's recent experience in Cambridge, the damage that it had done to his personal prospects, and the importance of his 'quitting [Aberdeen] with propriety and credit', one might expect him to have been a model subscriber to any library he patronised there. Yet some of his habits still seem, to a modern eye, surprisingly delinquent in their disregard for the physical integrity of the borrowed book or the library's exclusive authority over its consumption. Such traces of apparent delinquency offer an opportunity to reflect upon a relatively untouched topic: the ways in which library books of various sorts might have registered, with their users, as subject to fluid kinds of ownership, proprietorship, or, to appropriate Angus's term, 'custody'.

---

[209] Christopher Skelton-Foord estimates that novels and other duodecimo volumes usually incurred fines at 'a penny or two per day'. Skelton-Foord, 'Economics', 140–1.

[210] Varma, *The Evergreen Tree*, 50. Curiously, the recent study *Stealing Books in Eighteenth-Century London* does not contain any specific mention of books stolen from circulating libraries (Coulter, Mauger and Reid, *Stealing Books*).

At this point, a comparison is useful. When Charles stole ninety-two books from the University Library in Cambridge in 1777, his manner of defacing and hoarding them indicates that he clearly understood their status as stolen property. William Cole reports that Charles 'had taken the University Arms out of [the 35 books discovered in a dark corner of his room] & put his own in their place'. In 1962, J. C. T. Oates examined an identifiable eighty-four of the ninety-one volumes which Charles stole: 'The title-pages of nearly all the eighty-four identifiable volumes have been mutilated (and subsequently repaired). Class-marks have been cut away with scissors or erased, and some title-pages have been removed entire. A bookplate has been removed from inside the front board of most of the volumes, but portions of it remain in X.6.36 and X.12.28.'[211]

It seems that Charles's was a two-stage practice of reassigning ownership. The first step was to eradicate traces of library provenance by cutting with a blade, applying friction to fade the marks, or removing tell-tale pages entire. The second step was to superimpose a symbol of his own ownership – usually by gluing his own ex-libris, or bookplate, on the pastedown inside the front cover (see Figures 13 and 14). Of course, when Charles's theft was discovered and the books recovered, Cambridge librarians then tried to nullify the signs of ownership he had imposed. In two cases, they were not entirely successful; Figures 13 and 14 offer us rare evidence of Charles's superimpository practice.

In both cases, we can see that Charles pasted in a bookplate printed to a standardised design featuring a simple ornamental festoon overhanging the words 'Charles Burney, Cambridge'. Presumably – and poignantly – these had been commissioned by a proud father or family friend as a celebration of the young scholar's enrolment at the university. Charles's determination to put his stamp of ownership on the books makes it unlikely that, as Walker supposes, he stole them with the deliberate intention of selling them to pay his debts.[212] As a recent study of eighteenth-century book theft suggests, the ability to effect-ively 'launder' stolen second-hand books would be only hampered by traceable ownership inscriptions of any kind.[213] Instead, such activity indicates that he initially stole the books to keep, lending weight to Frances Burney's account of the motivation behind his crime – 'a Mad Rage for possessing a Library'.[214]

Brian Cummings and the Multigraph Collective have both recently con-sidered the role of bladed implements in relation to early modern printed books. The Multigraph Collective reads scissors as instruments of utility neces-sary to open the volume to perusal, whereas Cummings examines defacement, especially in relation to religious iconography, as the manifestation of

---

[211] Walker, 'Charles Burney's Theft', 326.   [212] Walker, 'Charles Burney's Theft', 324.

[213] Coulton, Mauger and Reid, *Stealing Books*, 95.

[214] Frances Burney to Charles Parr Burney, 26 February 1818, *JL* 10:795.

Figure 13 Remnants of Charles Burney's superimposed bookplate
in a stolen book (1).
Claudius Pulmanni, Ant. 1671, front pastedown, unpaginated. Cambridge, University of
Cambridge, Royal Library, X.6.36. Reproduced by kind permission of the Syndics of
Cambridge University Library.

'historical anger'.[215] Charles's approach to cutting books, though on one level
charged with a 'Mad Rage', is on another level eminently practical.[216] It reflects
the necessity of transferring them from one proprietorship (the University
Library's) to another (his own). Implicitly, therefore, the mere act of physically
removing the books from the library did not mean that they entered his custody.

---

[215] Cummings, *Bibliophobia*, 241.

[216] Multigraph Collective, *Interacting with Print,* 206. Frances Burney to Charles Parr Burney,
26 February 1818, *JL* 10:795.

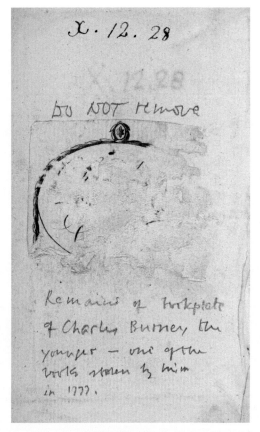

Figure 14 Remnants of Charles Burney's superimposed bookplate
in a stolen book (2).
Terentius, Lug. Bat., 1678. Front pastedown, unpaginated. Cambridge, University of
Cambridge, Royal Library, X.12.28. Reproduced by kind permission of the Syndics of
Cambridge University Library.

To 'possess' them, it was necessary to engage in violent and covert activity which, by means of excision and superimposition, attempted to reassign them as property.

Charles's documented treatments of the Aberdeen *Evelina* and the Banff *Evelina* are far more ambivalent. Unsurprisingly, given the mortifying consequences of his Cambridge transgression, we do not find evidence that he personally mutilated any of the volumes borrowed from Angus, or attached his own bookplate. However, he did, by his own admission, 'prefix' his sonnet to the novel, an enterprise which may well have involved paste or ink or both. Given Angus's injunction against 'damage', was this really within the spirit of subscription? We may find a partial answer in the vagueness of both Angus's and Charles's wording. Angus's reference in the *Conditions* to his patrons' temporary 'custody' of the novel, his offer of the opportunity to redress the offence by simply purchasing the book at its catalogue price, and his flexibility around 'reasonable . . . allowance', all indicate an inherent lack of confidence in his own permanent proprietorship over the books that made up his library. Similarly, the indeterminate character of Charles's verb 'prefix' might stand as a direct consequence of the liminal status of the book to which it was temporarily fastened. His act of temporary attachment reflects his status as a temporary 'custodian', to appropriate Angus's term, of the Aberdeen *Evelina*. Asserting custodianship with his (possibly signed) poetic paratext, he navigates the terrain between possession and appropriation in a manner that leaves its mark, as I argue here, in the very poetry he chose to prefix.

Charles's circulatory practice involves a similar tendency to ambivalent delinquency. We know from his declaration to Frances ('Before I return it') that he intended to return the book to Angus's, as prescribed by the *Conditions*. But was it really within the spirit of the rules to deliberately sublet a book so that a dozen or more readers could enjoy it for the price of one subscription? Here we are in little-charted territory, since the legal and behavioural status of subletting a circulating library book during this period has never quite been pinned down. Based on the patchy available evidence, there seems to have been a significant degree of variation as to how circulating library proprietors addressed such behaviour. Paul Kaufman suggests that borrowers from Thomas Wood's Shrewsbury circulating library were asked not to lend to non-subscribers.[217] Fergus finds evidence that a small number of borrowers in the Midlands 'declare' that a book will be read by other readers as well as themselves. Charlotte Stewart-Murphy notes anecdotal evidence from George Cheyne that 'each loan served a number of readers'.[218] Varma quotes a 1797 pamphlet, *The Use of Circulating Libraries Considered*, which describes subletting as 'ungenerous' and declares that it 'should, when known, be attended by the forfeit of the money paid for subscription'.[219] Overall, subletting seems to have been resented by proprietors but, since it could not be effectively monitored, grudgingly tolerated. Angus's silence on the practice, and the hints of weary resignation in the parenthetical 'when known' from the author of *The Use of Circulating Libraries*, seem to indicate as much.

Like proprietors, borrowers could also take a range of positions on the ethics of freeloading from a circulating library. If Frances Burney is to be believed, her brother was far from the only person who did this with *Evelina*. She reports an unnamed man reporting, 'there's no getting [*Evelina* . . .] the folks that hire it keep

---

[217] Kaufman, *Libraries and their Users*, 179.
[218] Stewart-Murphy, *A History of British Circulating-Libraries*, 30.
[219] Varma, *Evergreen Tree*, 200.

lending it from one to another in such a manner that it is never returned to the library. It's very provoking'.[220] Similarly, in his study of the visits made by Charlotte Francis (Charles and Frances Burney's niece, coincidentally) to a Brighton library in 1799, Stephen Colclough stresses the young woman's outrage at some friends who show 'meanness' in using library resources without subscribing, thereby 'transgress[ing] the social codes of a membership community'.[221]

Such activity, therefore, could be seen as 'provoking' or 'mean'. Despite this, Charles Burney does not seem remotely ashamed of his self-reported subletting practice at a moment when he had more reason to watch his step than most. We must assume too, unless Charles was able to misrepresent the book as his own,[222] that the eminently respectable citizens of Aberdeen who borrowed the book from him did not object too much to the practice of subletting either. Such participation acts as another hint that, during the period of the subscriber's 'custody' of a library book, the circulating library's proprietorship may have been felt to loosen or even be suspended altogether. Such hints, taken cumulatively, suggest that the university library and the commercial circulating library may have fostered very different senses of obligation in the same borrower, which in turn may have stimulated different treatments and behaviours of the borrowed books.

As Allan and Towsey both note, library records 'can only inform our understanding of the reading nation to a limited extent'.[223] Personal accounts like Charles's can help us to trace the footprint of borrowed books and to develop a sense – though, as both scholars stress, not a systematic one – of the impact of libraries on the reading nation.[224] Charles's practice should provoke us to reconsider how one loan may have spawned many readers, which might, in turn, lead us to recalibrate the likely scale of readership compared to book production or library holdings.[225] Where Kaufman calculates readership in terms of library borrowings with no explicit consideration of the fact that sublettings might have occurred, St Clair and Stewart-Murphy try to factor in a rough one-to-four multiplier.[226] Yet we see Charles Burney, empowered by his one-shilling-and-six-pence-per-month 'custody' of *Evelina* and with his own poetic preface framing it to the world, subletting Angus's set widely across

[220] Frances Burney to Susanna Elizabeth Burney, 12 October [1779], *EJL* 3:382.
[221] Charlotte Barrett, 'Journal of what passed in an excursion to Brighton', 16 August–23 September 1799, British Library, Western Manuscripts, Egerton MS 3706A, Ff 43r-34v. Qtd in Colclough, *Consuming Texts*, 95.
[222] This is unlikely, since it seems that Angus books generally contained a bookplate/advertisement. See Stewart-Murphy, *A History of British Circulating Libraries*, Plate II, unpaginated.
[223] Towsey, 'Store their minds', 570.
[224] Allan, *A Nation of Readers*, 214; Towsey, 'I can't resist', 17.
[225] Allan, *A Nation of Readers*, 214.
[226] Kaufman *Libraries and Their Users*, 196, 218; St. Clair, *The Reading Nation*, 235; Stewart-Murphy, *A History of British Circulating-Libraries*, 30.

households, to at least twelve readers and probably more. Such an example, though I make no claims for its representativeness, should inflect our sense of what circulating libraries made possible, both in terms of their demographic impact and their psychological weight.

5.2 'All the Sweet Creatures': Lending *Evelina*

Above, I suggest that the circulating library loan may have occupied a liminal proprietorial status in late eighteenth-century society, whereby it was perceived to enter the 'custody' of the borrower in such a way as to legitimate material and circulatory practices resembling those of an 'owned' volume. I now wish to nuance this argument by considering how such a status may have frustrated the ability of the borrower to undertake such practices. In previous sections, I have shown how Charles, deep in the throes of his identified performance of Macartney, attempted to use his sister's book and his own poetry to create a reading community (to appropriate Stephen Colclough's useful term) in which demonstrations of his literary prowess might be repaid by amatory and material advantage. I have also pinpointed his transmission of *Evelina* to his 'two angels, the Miss Willox's' as a particularly acute nexus of his amatory and material desires. When Charles addresses Jessy and Rachel, he has one foot in an established culture of gift-giving as 'an activity connecting patrons to their dependents' and the other in a newer one whereby exchange 'define[s] the intimate sphere'.[227] When we consider this loan within the context of Charles's temporary custodianship of the novel and the restrictions it imposed upon him, we start to understand how his status within a loan economy frustrated his efforts.

The amatory gift – what Charles Haskell Hinnant calls an 'erotically invested and investing performative' – has come under increased scrutiny in recent years with the renewed popularity of Marcel Mauss's anthropological work around gift exchange, the rise of material culture studies, and the 'turn' towards history of emotions. Sally Holloway provides a neat summary of the framing rationale. If 'the exchange of gifts was a crucial form of language', then it makes sense that exchanged objects 'played a fundamental role in creating and affirming feelings of love'. Holloway draws on Sara Ahmed's work on 'objects of happiness' to consider love tokens as 'sticky': 'they garner positive value as they are exchanged'.[228]

Books, of course, were one popular form of love token, which 'allowed lovers to gauge one another's reactions to particular texts and share their own reading preferences', acting as indicators of their 'education, disposition, and world view'. However, in a consumer marketplace where books were 'by nature standardised, identical, and available for anyone to purchase for a set price',

---

[227] Lynch, *Loving Literature*, 38.   [228] Holloway, *The Game of Love*, 14–16.

individuating strategies were often employed: 'Such objects held particular value if they had been adapted or modified by senders in some way, in order to render them unique.'[229] It is in this context that Andrew Piper has addressed personalised manuscript inscriptions included in Romantic miscellanies, arguing that they offered 'a way of replacing the anonymous distribution of mass-produced objects with a model of intimate circulation ... The discourse of friendship and the practice of gift-giving under which miscellanies were produced and circulated were intended to counteract precisely the anonymity of mass circulation'.[230]

I have argued that Charles's sonnet attempts to enforce a sentimental reading of the narrative that positions him as Macartney: poet, suppliant, brother, and lover. Given his declared romantic interest in Jessy Willox, in offering her the book with its carefully revised inscription (the reference to Orville removed, perhaps, so as not to dilute his performance of Macartney), he partially fulfils the terms of Holloway's definition, 'shar[ing] his own reading preferences" and 'gaug[ing]' Jessy's. However, crucially, his dedication to the 'Female Reader ... whoe'er thou art' is general rather than specific. The reason for this is both obvious and perplexing. Apparently oblivious to the imperative of the amatory gift to perform uniqueness, Charles did not intend that the book's subletting journey would stop with Jessy, since he wished to circulate it as widely as possible. The book's status as a loan is intrinsic to such logic, since, as Towsey points out, the act of borrowing 'decisively shape[s] ... reading of the books involved'.[231] Charles was borrowing Evelina from Angus to a timescale that was strictly demarcated, with a financial penalty for overdue returns. In terms of cost–benefit analysis, there was an imperative to eke out as much social capital as possible through an efficient subletting system and an even more efficient, because impersonal, dedication. In other words, Charles's indefinite language and indiscriminate practice are shaped by the temporary quality of his custodianship.

Such a strategy, of course, entirely misreads the defining quality of the amatory gift; it is supposed to be *special*. Perhaps unsurprisingly, therefore, Charles was unsuccessful in his attempt to create an amatory reading community. The sparse traces of Jessy Willox's reader response suggest that she spurned Charles's senti- mental dictum with considerable spirit. By his own account, she neither weeps nor sighs over the narrative, nor '[en]graves the moral' on her breast or heart. Instead, she resists Charles's call to sensibility by reading the novel as a comic romp, praising the vulgar Branghtons, declaring the boorish Captain Mirvan her 'favour- ite', and 'almost kill[ing] herself with laughing'.[232] In the face of Charles's gendered belletristic strictures, the violence of Jessy's laughter has a defiant quality.

---

[229] Holloway, *The Game of Love*, 98, 95, 117.   [230] Piper, 'The Art of Sharing', 131.
[231] Towsey, 'I can't resist', 214.
[232] Charles Burney to Frances Burney, OSB MSS 3, Box 6, Folder 381.

So too does the one poem of her composition that survives. Addressed to Charles a few months after he lent her *Evelina*, it both acknowledges a recent gift of some fruit, and acts as a broader response to his many poems:

> Since you're so fond of writing rhime,
> I just now think it proper time,
> You, in the same style to salute,
> And thank you for your fruit, you *Brute*.[233]

Amidst Charles's stock epithets and generic compliments, Jessy's energetic doggerel and irreverent banter are decidedly refreshing. She rejects the off-the-rack neoclassical terms imposed upon her, just as she rejects the reading of *Evelina* imposed by Charles's sonnet. Shortly afterwards she would deal the ultimate rejection: accepting the proposals of another suitor, John Campbell, while Charles was out of the way in Banff.

Jessy Willox, then, was not the Evelina to Charles's Macartney. Her older sister Rachel, however, who also borrowed the set, seems to have sympathised more with Charles's sentimental approach ('Miss Willox is very fond of [the character] Evelina'). Consequently, the correspondence suggests that Charles may have turned his attentions to Rachel over the later part of 1779 and early 1780. During this time, she, rather than Jessy, is the subject of Charles's most ambitious attempt to position himself as the broker of privileged access to the author of *Evelina*: a promise that he could persuade his celebrated sister to write to Rachel and eventually to meet her.

Charles apparently first approached Frances with this odd request in the early autumn of 1779. In October, Frances tells their father, 'I have written *my* long Letter to Charles, & taken what pains I could to show the imprudence of the request concerning a Commendatory Letter.'[234] Though she might reasonably refuse such a request simply on the grounds of not wanting to write an awkward note to someone she had never met, the reference to 'imprudence' indicates that she felt the act of writing the letter would in some way compromise either herself, or Charles, or both. However, Charles would not take no for an answer, and early the following year he tried to persuade Frances again. In an extant but badly mutilated letter, he laments that her refusal to write to Rachel 'grieves him much':

> On your engaging in a literary correspondence, till chance produced a meeting with my lovely friend, Miss Willox, I had set my heart – I am cruelly disappointed – Change your mind, I beseech you – ... Think [] pleasure you must receive from an epistolary correspondence with my Rachel, till you can be *vis a vis* with her.[235]

---

[233] Jessy Willox, 'Verses by Miss Jessy Willox, to thank C.B. for a present of Fruit', Osborn c37, 69.
[234] Frances Burney to Dr Charles Burney, 10 October [1779], *EJL* 3:360, n. 23.
[235] Charles Burney to Frances Burney [Feb/ March 1780], OSB MSS 3, Box 6, Folder 427.

The scope of Charles's request had apparently widened, by this time, from a 'Commendatory Letter' to a 'literary correspondence'. It seems likely that Frances ignored him; in any case, we hear no more of the request after this date.

Alongside the loan of *Evelina*, Charles's promise to 'my Rachel' can be read as another attempted amatory gift. Once again, his approach demonstrates a certain resourcefulness which, in place of financial credentials, offers celebrity connections and showcases literary pedigree. And, once again, his enterprise indicates only half an understanding of the conditions necessary for success. Just as he had with Jessy, Charles met with firm resistance from the woman whom he tried to fit to certain conceptual moulds to further his own ends. In this case, the resistance was that of his usually indulgent sister. Frances's staunch refusal to write to Rachel at Charles's request gives us a glimpse into how she may have viewed his other attempts to capitalise on her success.

The defining obligations of gift exchange, Marcel Mauss informs us, are to give, receive, and reciprocate.[236] A loan, however, creates the obligations to give, receive, and *return*: a crucial difference which, rather than taking the relationship between participants to new ground, moves it back to the starting position. It is certainly possible to envisage a context in which such a twice-gifting is actually conducive to courtship, enabling a palimpsestic emotional connection and re-connection over time, and fostering a reciprocity that the gift cannot achieve. Indeed, I have hinted that the annotation about moor fowl in the SC set of *Evelina* – which, we should remember, originally belonged to the Burney family rather than a library – may indicate precisely such a context. But Charles does not achieve this with his circulating library copy of *Evelina*. The temporary nature of the borrower's custody results in a frenetic rate of sublending, a temporary form of inscription, and a framing rhetoric of universality and indefiniteness which casts him as a deficient agent in the process of textual exchange.

There are, no doubt, many reasons for Charles Burney's failure to create his intended reading community. He was apparently just as clumsy a reader of women as he was of fiction, and it is likely that neither Jessy nor Rachel Willox took him seriously as a suitor. But it is important to note that Charles was operating within a loan economy dictated by his material circumstances as least as much as by his personal qualities. The book is not his own to give, merely an object that is temporarily in his 'custody'. It can be lent but it must also be reclaimed, a fact which is directly related to Charles's own financial precarity. Such a status in turn inflects his ability to mark the book effectively with his sonnet, or to convincingly address the 'sweet Creatures' whom he sought to target. He is hamstrung by his reliance on impersonal modes of circulation,

---

[236] Mauss, *The Gift*, 37.

address, and praise. In his cycle of lending and reclaiming his sister's novel, one can access a sense of his precarity in scholarly, sociable, familial, literary, and sexual spheres, and of the ways in which he attempted to exploit opportunities offered by print and manuscript cultures to bolster his own footing.

Afterword

On his return to London, Charles was cautiously welcomed back to the Burney household, though he spent the rest of 1781 lodging with relatives. An Aberdeen friend, Robert Burnside, probably helped him to secure a teaching post at a school in Highgate while he prepared to apply for ordination.[237] He was still in financial trouble; one of his last extant letters from 1781, to Findlater, 'earnestly beg[s]' for a loan of fifty guineas to 'settle his affairs', and it is unknown how he finally satisfied his creditors.[238] His woes were enhanced later in the year when the Bishop of London, responding to an anonymous tip-off about the Cambridge incident, refused to ordain him.[239] At the end of 1781, Charles's future did not look bright.

The year 1782 brought happier developments. Ironically, Charles's salvation eventually came in the shape of an advantageous marriage, the like of which he had pursued so ardently in Scotland. While working as a schoolmaster at the Chiswick private academy of William Rose (1719–86), he developed a mutual attachment with Rose's daughter Sarah (1759–1821) and married her in 1783. Shortly afterwards, when his father-in-law died, he stepped into the headmaster's shoes. The school proved successful under his stewardship, partly due to the fame he gradually achieved through his classical scholarship. Although the Cambridge theft continued to close doors to him for some time, his dual positions of educator and classicist were crucial to his eventual reputational rehabilitation and, at last, ordination at the age of fifty-one. The errors of his youth were often papered over by the strenuous efforts of his father, sister, and family friends to obtain patronage and career opportunities for him – more or less the role that he hoped Frances's book would play while he was in exile in Scotland.[240]

Such efforts were not one-sided. Regardless of his motivations or abilities, there is no doubt that Charles tried hard to advance the interests of his family members in return. He remained close to Frances for the rest of his life, and

---

[237] Burnside had a teaching position there: see his letters of 25 July and 27 August 1781 in OSB MSS 3. Box 3, Folder 158.

[238] Charles Burney to James Ogilvy, August 1781, OSB MSS 3, Box 7, Folder 452.

[239] *EJL* 4, p. 531, n. 61; 'Philalethes' to the Bishop of London, 5 December 1781, Caution Book of the Archbishops of Canterbury 1758–1785, Lambeth Palace Library, VO14-1

[240] For an account of Charles's career-building from 1781, see Walker, 'Charles Burney's Theft of Books at Cambridge'.

always took interest in promoting her literary productions to the extent that, from the 1790s onward, she consistently referred to him as her 'dear Agent'.[241] His heart, I think, always remained in the literary world, and especially in the theatre – he collected more than 300 volumes of extraordinary material towards a History of English Theatre, which he never managed to start writing. It is seldom noted that in 1795 he composed a ponderous poetic Prologue to Frances's tragedy *Edwy and Elgiva* and insisted that he be the one to 'exhibit' (read aloud) the play to the assembled cast for the first time in the Green Room at Drury Lane.[242] His desire to present Frances's creative work to the world through the lens of his own performance apparently remained unabated. Unfortunately, his exhibition embarrassed the actors, and the play itself was a disaster which closed after one performance.[243]

Despite the lack of sound judgement he often displayed at the nexus of sociable and literary activity, by the time Charles died in 1817, he boasted numerous honours and was by far the wealthiest of the Burneys.[244] He spent much of his disposable income at book auctions, amassing the 'Library' for which he had always had a 'Mad Rage'. At his death, this collection, comprising rare manuscripts and books, prints, news media, and theatrical materials, was purchased by Parliament and donated to the British Museum. In the parliamentary debate addressing its acquisition, ministers declared it 'peculiarly calculated for the Library of a Public Institution', predicted that it would provide 'a valuable encouragement to literature', and repeatedly compared it, in terms of value, to the Elgin Marbles.[245] Much (though not all) of the collection was transferred to the British Library in the 1970s. Today, in a small nod towards his importance as a collector, a glowering bust of Charles Burney oversees scholarly activity in the Manuscripts Reading Room at the St. Pancras site. In the dour expression captured by Joseph Nollekens, it is difficult to detect any trace of the juvenile criminal, the passionate lover, or the melancholy poet (See Figure 15).

About 200 years later, Charles's 'Library' has indeed had a significant cultural impact – especially (though perhaps unexpectedly) via his collection of early

[241] Frances Burney D'Arblay and Alexandre D'Arblay to Charles Burney, 17 June 1796, *JL* 3:168. See also Justice, *Manufactures of Literature,* 209; Salih, 'Camilla in the Marketplace', 122.

[242] For the Prologue see Charles Burney to Alexandre and Frances D'Arblay, 16 March 1795, Berg Coll MSS Arblay 196284B-287B, and Sabor, *The Complete Plays* 2:5, 2:13–14. For Hester Piozzi's excruciating account of Charles's reading, probably obtained from Sarah Siddons, see *Thraliana* 2: 916.

[243] Darby, *Frances Burney: Dramatist*, 53.

[244] Charles died inestate. After probate duty and administration, his estate (exclusive of real estate) was valued at just under £22,000 in 1819. See National Archives IR 26/207, Legacy Duty Record no 1234–1819, 'The Rev. Charles Burney'. I am grateful to John Avery Jones for helping me to locate the relevant legacy duty record.

[245] Anon, 'Imperial Parliament of Great Britain and Ireland', *Morning Chronicle*, 5 May 1818.

Figure 15 Abraham Wivell after Joseph Nollekens, 'The Rev.
Charles Burney D.D.'
Stipple engraving (London: J. Asperne for the *European Magazine,* 1819).
New Haven, Yale University, Beinecke Rare Book and Manuscript Library, The James
Marshall and Marie-Louise Osborn Collection Burney Family Collection, OSB MSS 3,
Box 7, Folder 493.

modern news ephemera, the largest in the world. Digitised on a subscription basis
by the e-research and educational publisher Gale Cengage, the Burney Collection
of Newspapers provides source material for an enormous amount of scholarly
research, across numerous disciplines, into the early modern period. As a result, it
is no exaggeration to say that Charles Burney's reading practices, and especially
his collecting habits, have had a powerful influence on several branches of the
humanities. Much remains to be done in reconstructing such practices, and
gauging their effects, in order to finally place Charles within scholarship around
collecting, crime, bibliomania, and the history of literary institutions.[246] This
Element has only been the first step.

---

[246] In *Stealing Books*, Coulton, Mauger and Reid devote only one glancing footnote to Charles's
theft (3). He is not mentioned in any of the chapters addressing bibliomania or collecting in
Ferris and Keen, *Bookish Histories.* The authoritative history of the British Library's printed
collections (Mandelbrote and Taylor, *Libraries within the Library*) contains no contribution
addressing the Burney Collection.

The story of *Evelina* in Aberdeen is fundamentally one about insecurity. At this moment in time, Charles Burney lacked confidence (often with good reason) in his security as a favoured child within his family unit, as a legitimated member of polite society, as an empowered agent within the print economy, and as a literary rival to his brilliant sister. In this Element, I have argued that such insecurity shapes, and is in turn shaped by, Charles's practices as a reader. Reading is often a self-interested act, undertaken for specific emotional and pragmatic purposes, which in turn creates consequential ripples far beyond the activity of perusing words on a page. Equally, I have shown that authorial celebrity like Frances Burney's does not emerge from a vacuum, nor even in any just and measured proportion to readerly pleasure or literary merit. Then, as now, it is an entity co-created by many different parties with a variety of interests and agendas.

Given that I attribute such insecurity to Charles, I want to acknowledge my own. Over the ten years during which I accumulated my evidence and constructed this case study, several spectres frequently haunted me. One was that of precipitate presumption. As a practicing writer of fiction as well as a scholar, I instinctively see the stories in archives, even when gaps and uncertainties exist. If one is not extremely careful to show one's working, tenuous connections and tendentious arguments can easily follow. I am acutely aware of the moments when I have gathered my courage and made a leap from a credible hypothesis to a tentative argument – around a poem which I have never seen, a set of indistinct 200-year-old marks on a page, the composition of a dateless fragment, or a cryptic doodle with infinite possible meanings. The 3D reading presented here represents a marriage between the rigour I try to practice as a scholar and the creative impulse which shapes my practice as a storyteller. I am apprehensive, but also curious and excited, to hear not only from readers who find my approach persuasive but also those who offer alternative views.

Another discomfiting spectre has been that of unrepresentativeness. To put it bluntly, the usefulness of my study might be perceived as limited, both because Charles Burney is not a typical reader and because his personal archive is unusually voluminous. How then can such an approach be more widely applied? Regarding the first hypothetical objection, I take solace in James Raven's approach to the topic. Where the 'distinctiveness' of such a 'micro-history' appears to 'highlight issues of representativeness', Raven recommends that we 'downplay the importance of broad uniformities, and . . . focus instead upon the qualitative differences of experience'.[247] As such, I have nowhere suggested that Charles Burney's reading practice should be taken as a blueprint for the average reader's in late eighteenth-century Britain. I merely suggest that

---

[247] Raven, *What Is the History of the Book?* 134–135.

we use it to consider the full range of possible experiences, and to exploit the whole range of interdisciplinary methodologies available.

Regarding the second objection, it is true that this wealth of archival evidence does not survive for the vast majority of eighteenth-century reading agents. I make no apology, but instead invite others to join me in the thriving interdisciplinary field of Burney studies, and to use what we have. It is no accident that some influential accounts of reading practice cited in this Element have already done so,[248] since the enormous, extraordinary archive of this family is unparalleled as a source for rich evidence of reading practices, and its surface has barely been scratched. As I have argued elsewhere, this archive results from a specific and rare combination of factors across several generations: excellent administrative skills, a considerable degree of self-importance, and a level of contemporary fame which made numerous family members noteworthy and their correspondence worth keeping.[249] Moreover, the groundbreaking recent scholarship of Amy Erickson and others suggests another quality which makes the archive not only rare but also unique. In beginning to uncover the plebeian trades, occupations, and connections that the Burneys' anxious editorial labours endeavoured for centuries to suppress, such scholarship has shown that the family spans a broader social milieu than was once imagined. Yes, the Burney family contained professors, courtiers, and clergy; but it also contained sailors, milliners, illiterate odd-job men, coffee-house proprietors, pawnbrokers, and criminals, as well as artists, musicians, and authors who often struggled to eke out a living. As I have shown, economic precarity and social anxiety often had effects on Burney identities and practices which simply cannot be found in the archives or libraries of more elite readers and writers.

In some respects, of course, this Element has inevitably raised more questions than it has answered. Charles's delinquent activity, sexuality, and finances all require more thorough scrutiny in order to account for some of his idiosyncrasies and achievements. It is my hope that one day a comprehensive edition of his c.2,500 extant letters – bolstered by an editorial apparatus informed by larger-scale 3D readings – will be able to tell a fuller story.

---

[248] Fergus, *Provincial Readers*; Colclough, *Consuming Texts*.

[249] Coulombeau, 'Introduction', *New Perspectives on the Burney Family*, 3.

Abbreviations

AJL Additional Journals and Letters of Frances Burney, general ed. Peter Sabor, 2 vols., Oxford, Oxford University Press, 2015–18.

EJL The Early Journals and Letters of Fanny Burney, general ed. Lars Troide, 5 vols., Oxford, Oxford University Press, 1988–2012.

JL The Journals and Letters of Fanny Burney (Madame D'Arblay), 1791–1840, ed. Joyce Hemlow *et al.*, 12 vols., Oxford, Clarendon Press, 1972–84.

LCB The Letters of Dr. Charles Burney, general ed. Peter Sabor, 6 vols., Oxford, Oxford University Press, 1991–present.

Bibliography

Anon., (1780). Answers to the Enigmas, *Ladies' Diary, or Woman's Almanack* 77 (1780), 15–16.

Anon., (1775). Mathematical Correspondence, *London Magazine, or Gentleman's Monthly Intelligencer*, 44 (August 1775), 417.

Anon., (1779). Mathematical Correspondence, *London Magazine, or Gentleman's Monthly Intelligencer*, 48 (January 1779), 34.

Anon., (1779). *A new catalogue of the Aberdeen Circulating Library, consisting of several thousand volumes . . .*, Aberdeen: Alexander Angus. University of Aberdeen, (SC) SBL 1779 NP 2.

Anon., (1818). Imperial Parliament of Great Britain and Ireland, *Morning Chronicle* [1801], 5 May 1818. British Library Newspapers, link.gale.com/apps/doc/BB3207279401/BNCN?u= uniyork&sid=bookmark-BNCN. Accessed 15 March 2023.

Allan, David (2008). *A Nation of Readers: The Lending Library in Georgian England*, London: British Library.

Alston, Robin (2006). 'Libraries in Scotland to 1850', Scribd, uploaded by Andrew Prescott 19 July 2006, accessed 26 July 2023. www.scribd.com/document/63097322/Robin-Alston-Library-History-Scotland, https://data.cerl.org/sbti/000738.

Austen, Jane (2004). *Persuasion*, ed. James Kinsley, intr. Deidre Shauna Lynch. Oxford: Oxford University Press.

Balderston, Katharine C. (1942). *Thraliana: The Diary of Mrs. Hester Lynch Thrale, 1776–1809*, 2 vols., Oxford: Clarendon Press.

Bander, Elaine (2021). 'The Astronomic Muse: Charles Burney and Astronomy', *Journal for Eighteenth-Century Studies*, 44:3 (September 2021), 259–276.

Bannet, Eve Tavor (2017). *Eighteenth-Century Manners of Reading: Print Culture and Popular Instruction in the Anglophone Atlantic World*, Cambridge: Cambridge University Press.

Burney, Frances (1779). *Evelina: Or, the History of a Young Lady's Entrance into the World*, 3 vols. London: Thomas Lowndes, 1779 (3rd ed.). University of Aberdeen, SB 82366 E1.

Burney, Frances (2002). *Evelina: Or, the History of a Young Lady's Entrance into the World*, ed. Edward A. Bloom, intr. Vivian Jones, Oxford: Oxford University Press.

Burney, Frances (2008). *Cecilia: Or, Memoirs of an Heiress*, ed. Peter Sabor and Margaret Anne Doody, intr. Margaret Anne Doody. Oxford: Oxford University Press.

Certeau, Michel de (1988). 'Reading as Poaching', *The Practice of Everyday Life*, trans. Steven Rendall, Berkeley, Los Angeles: University of California Press. Reproduced in Towheed et al., 2011, 130–139.

Chisholm, Kate (1998). *Fanny Burney: Her Life (1752–1840)*, London: Chatto & Windus.

Clark, Lorna J., (2020–21). 'Growing up Burney, and the Role of a Commonplace Book', *Journal of Juvenilia Studies*, 3:1, 3–20.

Colclough, Stephen (2007). *Consuming Texts: Readers and Reading Communities, 1695–1870*. London: Palgrave Macmillan.

Coulombeau, Sophie (2018). 'Introduction', *New Perspectives on the Burney Family*, special issue of *Eighteenth-Century Life*, 42:2, 1–13.

Coulton, Richard, Mauger, Matthew and Reid, Christopher (2016). *Stealing Books in Eighteenth-Century London*, London: Palgrave Macmillan.

Cummings, Brian (2021). *Bibliophobia: The End and the Beginning of the Book*, Oxford: Oxford University Press.

Dale, Amelia (2022). 'The Quixotic Eighteenth Century', *Literature Compass*, 19:5.

Darby, Barbara (1997). *Frances Burney, Dramatist: Gender, Performance, and the Late Eighteenth-Century Stage*, Lexington: University of Kentucky Press.

Dingwall Fordyce, Alexander (1885). *Family Record of the Name of Dingwall Fordyce in Aberdeenshire . . .*, Toronto: C. Blackett Robinson.

Doody, Margaret A. (1988). *Frances Burney: The Life in the Works*, New Brunswick: Rutgers University Press.

Eger, Elizabeth and Peltz, Lucy (2008). *Brilliant Women: Eighteenth-Century Bluestockings*, New Haven: Yale University Press.

Ellis, Markman (2013). 'Reading Practices in Elizabeth Montagu's Epistolary Network of the 1750s', *Bluestockings Displayed: Portraiture, Performance and Patronage, 1730–1830*, Cambridge: Cambridge University Press, 213–232.

Erickson, Amy (2018). 'Esther Sleepe, Fan-Maker, and Her Family', *Eighteenth-Century Life* 42:2, 15–37.

Fergus, Jan (2007). *Provincial Readers in Eighteenth-Century England*, Oxford: Oxford University Press.

Ferris, Ina and Keen, Paul (2009). *Bookish Histories: Books, Literature and Commercial Modernity*, London: Palgrave Macmillan.

Fox, Adam (2020). *The Press and the People: Cheap Print and Society in Scotland, 1500–1785*, Oxford: Oxford University Press.

Gallagher, Catherine (1994). *Nobody's Story: The Vanishing Acts of Women Writers in the Marketplace, 1670–1920*. Berkeley: University of California Press.

Genette, Gérard (1997). *Paratexts: Thresholds of Interpretation*, trans. Jane E. Lewey, foreword by Richard Macksey. Cambridge: Cambridge University Press.

Goetsch, Paul (2004). 'Reader Figures in Narrative', *Style*, 38:2, 188–202.

Griffin, Dustin (1996). *Literary Patronage in England, 1650–1800*, Cambridge: Cambridge University Press.

Halsey, Katie (2012). *Jane Austen and Her Readers, 1786–1945*, London: Anthem.

Harvey, Arnold D., (2001). *Sex in Georgian England: Attitudes and Prejudices from the 1720s to the 1820s*, London: George Duckworth.

Havens, Hilary (2016). Maria Edgeworth's (Deleted) Thoughts on Frances Burney's *Evelina*, *Aphra Behn Online Public: An Interactive Forum for Women in the Arts, 1640–1830*, 7 October 2016, https://web.archive.org/web/20180331004915/http://www.aphrabehn.org/ABO/maria-edgeworths-deleted-thoughts-on-frances-burneys-evelina/.

Havens, Hilary (2019). *Revising the Eighteenth-Century Novel: Authorship from Manuscript to Print*, Cambridge: Cambridge University Press.

Hemlow, Joyce (1958). *The History of Fanny Burney*, Oxford: Clarendon Press.

Hemlow, Joyce. (1972–1984). *The Journals and Letters of Fanny Burney (Madame d'Arblay), 1791–1840*, 12 vols. Oxford: Clarendon Press.

Hinnant, Charles Haskell (2009). 'The Erotics of the Gift: Gender and Exchange in the Eighteenth-Century Novel', in Linda Zionkowski and Cynthia Klekar, eds., *The Culture of the Gift in Eighteenth-Century England*, London: Palgrave Macmillan, 143–158.

Holloway, Sally (2019). *The Game of Love in Georgian England: Courtship, Emotions, and Material Culture*, Oxford: Oxford University Press.

Jacob, William (2007). *The Clerical Profession in the Long Eighteenth Century, 1680–1840*, Oxford: Oxford University Press.

Jackson, Heather (2002). *Marginalia: Readers Writing in Books*, New Haven: Yale University Press, 2002.

Johnson, Samuel (2021). *A Dictionary of the English Language*, 1755, 1773. Edited by Beth Rapp Young, Jack Lynch, William Dorner, Amy Larner Giroux, Carmen Faye Mathes, and Abigail Moreshead et al. https://johnsons dictionaryonline.com.

Justice, George (2002). *The Manufacturers of Literature: Writing and the Literary Marketplace in Eighteenth-Century England*, Newark: University of Delaware Press.

Kaufman, Paul (1969). *Libraries and Their Users: Collected Papers in Library History*, London: the Library Association.

Kochkina, Svetlana (2023). *Frances Burney's Evelina: The Book, Its History, and Its Paratext*, Cham: Palgrave Macmillan.

Koehler, Martha J. (2005). *Models of Reading: Paragons and Parasites in Richardson, Burney, and Laclos*, Lewisburg: Bucknell University Press.

Krawczyk, Scott (2009). *Romantic Literary Families*, London: Palgrave Macmillan.

Lanning, Katie (2020). 'Scanner Darkly: Unpopularization in the Burney Newspaper Collection', *Archives and Records*, 41(3), 215–235.

Lawrance, Robert Murdock (1923). *An Old Book-Selling Firm: Alexander Angus & Son*, Aberdeen: D.Wylie & Son.

Levy, Michelle (2008). *Family Authorship and Romantic Print Culture*, London: Palgrave Macmillan.

Lough, J. and M. (1945). 'Aberdeen Circulating Libraries in the Eighteenth Century', *Aberdeen University Review* 31, 17–23.

Lynch, Deidre Shauna (2014), *Loving Literature: A Cultural History*, Chicago: University of Chicago Press.

Mandelbrote, Giles and Taylor, Barry (2009). *Libraries within the Library: The Origins of the British Library's Printed Collections*, London: British Library.

Matthews, Charley (2022). '"I Feel the Mind Enlarging Itself": Anne Lister's Gendered Reading Practices', *Journal of Lesbian Studies*, 26:4, 367–381.

Matthews, Charley (2023). '"To Do a Little and Well": Anne Lister's Reading Routine', *Reception: Texts, Readers, Audiences, History*, 15, 25–31.

Mauss, Marcel (1970). *The Gift: Forms and Functions of Exchange in Archaic Societies*, trans. Ian Cunnison, London: Cohen & West.

McDonald, William R. (1968). Circulating Libraries in the North-East of Scotland in the Eighteenth Century, *Bibliotheck*, 5,119–137.

Mee, John, and Matthew Sangster, 'Introduction', *Institutions of Literature, 1700–1900*, Cambridge: Cambridge University Press, 1–23.

Michaelson, Patricia Howell (2002). *Speaking Volumes: Women, Reading and Speech in the Age of Austen*, Stanford: Stanford University Press.

Nedobity, Wolfgang (2007). 'Lord Findlater and His Impact on Continental Landscaping', 23 July 2007. SSRN: https://ssrn.com/abstract=1172282 or http://dx.doi.org/10.2139/ssrn.1172282.

Päckert, Martin, and Frank Klyne (2022). *Lord Findlater und die Gärten seiner Zeit: Mehrdeutigkeiten eines Lebens und einer Kunstform*, Darmstadt: wbg Academic.

Paluchowska-Messing, Anna (2020). *Frances Burney and Her Readers: The Negotiated Image*, Berlin: Peter Lang.

Peake, Richard Brinsley (1841). *Memoirs of the Colman Family: Including Their Correspondence with the Most Distinguished Personages of Their Time*, 2 vols, London: Richard Bentley.

Pearson, David (2019). *Provenance Research in Book History: A Handbook*, Oxford: Bodleian Library, 2019.

Piper, Andrew (2009). 'The Art of Sharing: Reading in the Romantic Miscellany', in Ina Ferris and Paul Keen, eds., *Bookish Histories: Palgrave Studies in the Enlightenment, Romanticism and Cultures of Print*, London: Palgrave Macmillan, 126–147.

Raven, James (2018). *What Is the History of the Book?*, Cambridge: Polity Press.

Raven, James, Helen Small and Naomi Tadmor (2007). *The Practice and Representation of Reading in England*, Cambridge: Cambridge University Press.

Rennhak, Katharina (2011). 'Paratexts and the Construction of Author Identities: The Preface as Threshold and Thresholds in the Preface', in Karremann, Isabel and Muller, Anja, eds., *Mediating Identities in Eighteenth-Century England: Public Negotiations, Literary Discourses, Topography*, Kent: Ashgate Publishing, 55–70.

Readioff, Corinna (2021). 'Recent Approaches to Paratext Studies in Eighteenth-Century Literature', *Literature Compass*, 18:12.

Richardson, Samuel (1776). *The History of Sir Charles Grandison, in a Series of Letters*, 8 vol. London: John Donaldson.

Ritter, Richard de (2014). *Imagining Women Readers*, Manchester: Manchester University Press.

Russell, Gillian (2020). *The Ephemeral Eighteenth Century: Print, Sociability, and the Cultures of Collecting*, Cambridge: Cambridge University Press.

Sabor, Peter, ed. (1995). *The Complete Plays of Frances Burney*, 2 vols., London: Pickering & Chatto, 1995.

Sabor, Peter, ed. (2015-8). *Additional Journals and Letters of Frances Burney*, 2 vols., Oxford: Oxford University Press.

Sabor, Peter, ed. (1991–). *The Letters of Dr. Charles Burney*, 6 vols., Oxford, Oxford University Press.

Sabor, Peter, ed. (2018). 'The March of Intimacy: Dr Burney and Dr Johnson', *Eighteenth-Century Life* 42:2, 38–55.

Saggini, Francesca (2012). *Backstage in the Novel: Frances Burney and the Theater Arts*, Charlottesville: University of Virginia Press.

Salih, Sarah (2002). 'Camilla in the Marketplace: Moral Marketing and Feminist Editing in 1796 and 1802', in Emma Clery, Caroline Franklin, and

Peter Garside, eds., *Authorship, Commerce and the Public: Scenes of Writing, 1750–1830*. Houndmills: Palgrave Macmillan, 120–135,

Schellenberg, Betty A. (2016). *Literary Coteries and the Making of Modern Print Culture, 1740–1790*. Cambridge: Cambridge University Press.

Scholes, Percy (1948). *The Great Dr Burney: His Life, His Travels, His Works, His Family and His Friends*, 2 vols., Oxford: Oxford University Press.

Sherwood, George Frederick Tudor (1908). *The Pedigree Register*, 2 vols., London: Society of Genealogists.

Skelton-Foord, Christopher (2002). 'Economics, Expertise, Enterprise and the Literary Scene: The Commercial Management Ethos in Circulating Libraries, 1780–1830', in Emma Clery, Caroline Franklin, and Peter Garside, eds., *Authorship, Commerce and the Public: Scenes of Writing, 1750–1830*, Houndmills: Palgrave Macmillan, 136–152.

Sol, Antoinette (2002). *Textual Promiscuities: Eighteenth-Century Critical Rewriting*, Lewisburg: Bucknell University Press.

Spencer, Jane (2005). *Literary Relations: Kinship and the Canon 1660–1830*, Oxford: Oxford University Press.

St. Clair, William (2004). *The Reading Nation in the Romantic Period*, Cambridge: Cambridge University Press.

Stephen, James (1954). *The Memoirs of James Stephen, Written by Himself for the Use of His Children*, ed. Merle M. Bevington, London: Hogarth Press.

Stewart-Murphy, Charlotte (1992). *A History of British Circulating Libraries: The Book Labels and Ephemera of the Papantonio Collection*, Newtown: Bird & Bull Press.

Tayler, Alastair and Henrietta (1925). *Lord Fife and His Factor, Being the Correspondence of James Second Lord Fife 1729–1809*, London: William Heinemann.

The Multigraph Collective (2018). *Interacting with Print: Elements of Reading in the Era of Print Saturation*, Chicago: University of Chicago Press.

Towheed, Shafquat, Rosalind Crone and Katie Halsey (2011). *The History of Reading: A Reader*, London: Routledge.

Towsey, Mark (2010). *Reading the Scottish Enlightenment: Books and Their Readers in Provincial Scotland, 1750–1820*, Leiden: Brill.

Towsey, Mark (2013). 'I Can't Resist Sending You the Book: Private Libraries, Elite Women, and Shared Reading Practices in Georgian Britain', *Library & Information History*, 29:3, 210–222.

Towsey, Mark (2015). 'Store Their Minds with Much Valuable Knowledge: Agricultural Improvement at the Selkirk Subscription Library, 1799–1814', *Journal for Eighteenth-Century Studies* 38:4, 569–584.

Troide, Lars, ed. (1988–2012). *The Early Journals and Letters of Fanny Burney*, 5 vols. Oxford: Oxford University Press.

Varma, Devendra P. (1972). *The Evergreen Tree of Diabolical Knowledge*, Washington, DC: Consortium Press.

Walker, Ralph (1962). 'Charles Burney's Theft of Books at Cambridge', *Transactions of the Cambridge Bibliographical Society*, iii, 313–326.

Walker, Ralph (1973). 'Charles Burney's Tour in the North-East of Scotland', 1780, *Aberdeen University Review*, XLV, 1:149, 1–19.

Whitehead, Angus (2006). 'A Various Complicated Ill: Echoes of Cotton and Cowley in *Evelina*', *Notes and Queries*, 53:3, 309–310.

Williams, Abigail (2017). *The Social Life of Books: Reading Together in the Eighteenth-Century Home*, New Haven: Yale University Press.

Williams, Abigail (2023). *Reading It Wrong: An Alternative History of Early Eighteenth-Century Literature*, Princeton: Princeton University Press.

Manuscript Collections Referenced

Burney Family Collection, The James Marshall and Marie-Louise Osborn Collection, Beinecke Rare Book and Manuscript Library, Yale University, New Haven. OSB MSS 3.

Catalogues / lists, Library Administration, Library, Kings College Archives, University of Aberdeen Special Collections. GB 0231, KINGS 5/1/1.

Caution Book of the Archbishops of Canterbury 1758–1785, Lambeth Palace Library. VO14-1.

Collection of Commonplace Books (I. Epigrams), Houghton Library, Harvard University, Cambridge, Mass. MS Eng 926.

Elizabeth Carter and Hannah More Letters to Mary Hamilton, Houghton Library, Harvard University, Cambridge, Mass. MS Eng 1778.

Frances Burney d'Arblay Collection of Papers. Henry W. and Albert A. Berg Collection of English and American Literature, The New York Public Library, Astor, Lennox and Tilden Foundations. Berg Coll MSS Arblay.

National Archives, Death duties 1796–1903, IR 26.

Papers relating to Duff family of Duff House, William Rose of Montcoffer, Factor and Hay of Rannes (Lumley-Smith papers), University of Aberdeen Special Collections. MS 997.

Papers of the Duff family of Duff House, and William Rose of Montcoffer, Their Factor, University of Aberdeen Special Collections. MS 2226.

The James Marshall and Marie-Louise Osborn Collection, Beinecke Rare Book and Manuscript Library, Yale University, New Haven. Osborn c6, Osborn c35, Osborn c37, Osborn c6, Osborn c 38.

Digital Projects Referenced

Books and Borrowing: An Analysis of Scottish Readers' Registers 1750–1830. 2020–2024. University of Stirling. Project funded by the Arts & Humanities Research Council (Ref.AH/T003960/1). https://borrowing.stir.ac.uk

Libraries, Reading Communities & Cultural Formation in the 18th Century Atlantic. 2019–2024. University of Liverpool. Project funded by the Arts & Humanities Research Council (Ref.AH/S007083/). https://c18librarieson line.org/

The French Book Trade in Enlightenment Europe Project, 1769–1794. 2015–present. University of Leeds & Western Sydney University. Project funded by the Arts & Humanities Research Council (Ref. AH/E509363/1) and Western Sydney University. http://fbtee.uws.edu.au/stn/.

READ-IT (Reading Europe Advanced Data Investigation Tool). 2018–2021. Université du Main le Mans. Project funded by the Joint Programming Initiative for Cultural Heritage (JPICH, Ref. 335-54-103). https://readit-project.eu/.

Unlocking the Mary Hamilton Papers. 2019–2023. University of Manchester. Project funded by the Arts & Humanities Research Council (Ref. AH/S007121/1), https://www.maryhamiltonpapers.alc.manchester.ac.uk/.

Acknowledgements

I am indebted to the Burney Centre and the American Society for Eighteenth-Century Studies for awarding me the 2013 ASECS-Mcgill Fellowship, during which my curiosity about Charles Burney was first ignited. That interest has since been fostered by mentors and friends associated with the Centre, including Peter Sabor, Stewart Cooke, Elaine Bander, Ann Marie Holland, Richard Virr, and Svetlana Kochkina. I deeply appreciate their expertise and generosity. Thanks to the Burney Society for providing a rich environment for discussion and debate, especially Lorna Clark, Francesca Saggini, Hilary Havens, Cassie Ulph, Gillian Skinner, Alison Daniell, Miriam Al-Jamil, Trudie Messent, Michael Burney-Cumming, and Paula Stepankowsky.

I am grateful to the Society of Scottish Antiquaries for awarding me a grant to visit the University of Aberdeen in 2022, to Mark Towsey for endorsing my application, and to Michelle Gait, Jan Smith, Lisa Collinson, and Janet Cruikshank for supporting my research. I am grateful to Cardiff University for funding a 2016 trip to New Haven to examine Charles Burney's manuscript letters and poetry, and to the helpful staff at the Beinecke Library. Special thanks to Alice Kelly for coming to the rescue. The later stages of this project could not have been completed without generous support from the Department of English and Related Literature and the Centre for Eighteenth-Century Studies at the University of York.

During the decade that this little book has been gestating, I have profited from conversations with Harriet Guest, John Barrell, Kevin Gilmartin, Felicity Nussbaum, Anthony Mandal, Chloe Wigston-Smith, Devoney Looser, Gillian Dow, Gillian Russell, David O'Shaughnessy, Fiona Ritchie, Jennie Batchelor, Deidre Lynch, Amy Erickson, Ruth Scobie, Mascha Hansen, Jon Mee, Mary Fairclough, Emma Major, Jim Watt, Alison O'Byrne, Olivia Carpenter, Deborah Russell, Joanna Wharton, Harrie Neal, Helen Metcalfe, Helen Smith, Brian Cummings, Freya Sierhuis, Juliana Mensah, David Harper, Emilie Morin, Dan Waterfield, James Raven, Hannah Barker, Chris Stray, Mark Towsey, Katie Halsey, Matt Sangster, Wolfgang Neobity, Martin Päckert, Frank Klyne, David Denison, Nuria Yañez-Bouza, Christine Wallis, Tino Oudesluijs, Zachary Lesser, Natasha Simonova, Liz Edwards, Giles Mandelbrote, John Avery Jones, Tanya Kirk, and Maddy Smith. Lorna Clark generously provided a fresh set of (expert) eyes at a crucial moment. Emilie Morin and Peter Sabor provided valuable feedback on the finished manuscript. Rich Hardiman's design skills and customer service remain, as ever, unparalleled.

For permission to use images, I must thank the Beinecke, the University of Aberdeen's Special Collections, Rare Books and Special Collections at McGill, the British Museum, and Cambridge University Library. I am grateful to Markman Ellis, Eve Tavor Bannet, Bethany Thomas and her colleagues, and the anonymous peer reviewers for helping me to improve my work. The University of York provided the funds to publish this Element so that it is freely accessible to all.

Heartfelt gratitude to my mum Noëlla for her weekly visits, to my husband Rich for his omnipresence at the school gates, and to Tilly for the perspective.

For Tilly, my other litel boke.

Cambridge Elements ⁼

Eighteenth-Century Connections

Series Editors

Eve Tavor Bannet
University of Oklahoma

Eve Tavor Bannet is George Lynn Cross Professor Emeritus, University of Oklahoma and editor of *Studies in Eighteenth-Century Culture*. Her monographs include *Empire of Letters: Letter Manuals and Transatlantic Correspondence 1688–1820* (Cambridge, 2005), *Transatlantic Stories and the History of Reading, 1720–1820* (Cambridge, 2011), and *Eighteenth-Century Manners of Reading: Print Culture and Popular Instruction in the Anglophone Atlantic World* (Cambridge, 2017). She is editor of *British and American Letter Manuals 1680–1810* (Pickering & Chatto, 2008), *Emma Corbett* (Broadview, 2011) and, with Susan Manning, *Transatlantic Literary Studies* (Cambridge, 2012).

Markman Ellis
Queen Mary University of London

Markman Ellis is Professor of Eighteenth-Century Studies at Queen Mary University of London. He is the author of *The Politics of Sensibility: Race, Gender and Commerce in the Sentimental Novel* (1996), *The History of Gothic Fiction* (2000), *The Coffee-House: a Cultural History* (2004), and *Empire of Tea* (co-authored, 2015). He edited *Eighteenth-Century Coffee-House Culture* (4 vols, 2006) and *Tea and the Tea-Table in Eighteenth-Century England* (4 vols 2010), and co-editor of *Discourses of Slavery and Abolition* (2004) and *Prostitution and Eighteenth-Century Culture: Sex, Commerce and Morality* (2012).

Advisory Board

Linda Bree, *Independent*
Claire Connolly, *University College Cork*
Gillian Dow, *University of Southampton*
James Harris, *University of St Andrews*
Thomas Keymer, *University of Toronto*
Jon Mee, *University of York*
Carla Mulford, *Penn State University*
Nicola Parsons, *University of Sydney*
Manushag Powell, *Purdue University*
Robbie Richardson, *University of Kent*
Shef Rogers, *University of Otago*
Eleanor Shevlin, *West Chester University*
David Taylor, *Oxford University*
Chloe Wigston Smith, *University of York*
Roxann Wheeler, *Ohio State University*
Eugenia Zuroski, *MacMaster University*

About the Series

Exploring connections between verbal and visual texts and the people, networks, cultures and places that engendered and enjoyed them during the long Eighteenth Century, this innovative series also examines the period's uses of oral, written and visual media, and experiments with the digital platform to facilitate communication of original scholarship with both colleagues and students.

Cambridge Elements ≡

Eighteenth-Century Connections

Elements in the Series

A full series listing is available at: www.cambridge.org/EECC

Printed in the United States
by Baker & Taylor Publisher Services